Livengoods Living Well

Livengoods Living Well

Douglas W. Price

Livengoods Living Well

© Douglas W. Price 2025

This book is a work of fiction. Named locations are used fictitiously, and characters and incidents are the product of the author's imagination. Any resemblance to actual events or places or persons, living or dead, is entirely coincidental.

All rights reserved. Without limiting the rights under copyright reserved above, no part of this publication may be reproduced, stored in a retrieval system, or transmitted, in any form or by any means (electronic, mechanical, photocopying, recording or otherwise), without the prior written permission of the copyright owner of this book.

Published by
Lighthouse Christian Publishing
SAN 257-4330
5531 Dufferin Drive
Savage, Minnesota, 55378
United States of America

www.lighthousechristianpublishing.com

For Mom, Dad, Lynne
Patricia
Christina, Bernadette, Margaret
Tim & Aunt Tu

Table of Contents

Part 1 Who Am I? A look Inside

Chapter One – A Full Heart…………………………1

Chapter Two – Happy Just the Way I Am…………..6

Chapter Three –
Growing While They're Learning…………………...10

Chapter Four – I Have Dignity………………………15

Chapter Five – What a Team!..................................21

Chapter Six – Peaceful………………………………..26

Chapter Seven – The Gift of a Full Heart…………...29

Chapter Eight – Good Company……………………36

Chapter Nine – Look Deep Within…………………..40

Part II Who Are We? – Standing Together

Chapter One – Together and Within………………..44

Chapter Two – A Full Heart for Max Again………..48

Chapter Three – Sunny and Bright…………………54

Chapter Four – Relief and Happiness………………58

Chapter Five – "To Life!"……………………………62

Chapter Six – A Story Ended…………………………..66

Chapter Seven – Getting Better, Getting Worse……70

Chapter Eight – Standing Together…………………..74

Chapter Nine – Well on the Way Home……………..78

Part III – We Rise – Stamina and Stability

Chapter One – So Much to Do, So Little Time……...83

Chapter Two – A Good Advice Team………………..90

Chapter Three – What a Day!..95

Chapter Four – "Truth to Me"………………………..102

Chapter Five – A Foundation…………………………109

Chapter Six – Wonderful to Behold………………...119

Chapter Seven – From a Full Heart………………...126

Chapter Eight –
Tears and Laughter in God's Eye…………………..132

Chapter Nine – The Living Well Conference………140

Author's note

Part I follows a boy and a girl from early childhood into young adulthood as they grow to resolve typical issues of personal identity as well as practices and beliefs of increasingly widespread acceptance that challenge our Christian beliefs and heritage as well as age-old norms for human behavior.

A chapter is given to every two years in their lives with an orientation to traditional values, but with very clear statements from the main characters supporting kindness, support, and generosity for those with different beliefs and ways of living.

Vocabulary, sentence structure and length, and content vary by chapter according to the ages of the main characters. Chapters one through three may be read to or with children ages 3-9, chapters four through six ages 9-13, chapters seven through nine are for ages 15-21. Those without children may like to accompany Donald and Linda in their formative stages of growth.

Parts II and III are intended for young adults through readers in their elder years. Opportunities and challenges of personal growth and developing durable relationships test and develop the integrity of each character, always with the prevailing wisdom of Christian beliefs, moral values, and ethics.

Author's Background

In his almost 50 years in education, the author has worked in public, private, charter, and parochial schools. He has been a teacher in elementary, middle, high school and college and has taught children as young as three and adults of all ages into their fifties. He has been a publisher's representative and worked in private industry presenting and developing educational programs and materials. He has taught in rural and urban areas and in jail. He was an elementary principal for 21 years. He believes "Education at its best is an adventure."

Douglas W. Price

Part I -- Who Am I, a Look Inside

Chapter One – A Full Heart

The doorbell rang at the small brick house of Mr. and Ms. Livengood and Donald, five years old, and Linda, three. Shadow ran to the door and barked. When she saw it was Aunt Tu, she became excited and wagged her tail. Aunt Tu lived far away, traveled a lot, and only visited every two years, but Shadow seemed to remember her. When Linda was only a year old, Aunt Tu had said to her, "I am a mother, too," and Linda and David called her Aunt Tu from then on.

She always brought something for the children, and this time it was wrapped in silver paper.

They all gave their aunt a big hug with true smiles. Shadow licked her and ran around the house in all the excitement. Aunt Tu was very happy to be with them all again.

When the children unwrapped the present, they saw it was a small book. Dad read the title: Who Am I, A Look Inside.

"I know who I am; I am Donald."

"I am Linda," said his sister.

"Yes, you are," replied their father. "And we are very happy that you are our son and daughter!"

"This story begins with a song. You know the tune of *If You're Happy and You Know It, Clap Your Hands* so you can sing along, but these are different words for you to learn. Let's hum it a couple of times first."

Mr. and Ms. Livengood and the children hum the song. It takes Linda just a little while longer because she is younger, but soon they both have it.

"Now here are the words from the book," says Mom. I'll read them, then I'll sing them to the tune you know, then we'll all sing them together.

Yes, I am me; I really am. Let's clap hands. (clap, clap, clap)
These are my eyes and both my hands. Let's clap hands. (clap, clap, clap)

"As you sing the word eyes, touch them. When you sing 'hands', wave them," says Mom.

The family sings these lines. The children do very well.

"Mom and Dad and Aunt Tu will sing these words for you, and you repeat them." Mom points to the words as she reads them, then the grown-ups sing with the children repeating each line.

Whenever I sing my own song, I know for sure I can't go wrong,
All together let's sing this song; let's clap hands. (clap, clap, clap)

"You did that very well, Mom says. "Now we will sing the rest of the song, and you repeat the words for each line again. Later we'll help you learn all of the words. In the meantime, practice just the first four lines so you can remember and sing that much by yourselves whenever you want. Donald, please read the words to Linda until she knows them." Mom and Dad and Aunt Tu sing and include hand movements. Donald and Linda repeat the words. They really are getting pretty good at this.

These are my eyes and this my nose. Let's clap hands. (clap, clap, clap)

I'm going to wiggle all my toes. Let's clap hands. (clap, clap, clap)

Linda and Donald laugh as they wiggle their toes.

Whenever I sing my own song, I know for sure I can't go wrong.

All together let's sing this song. Let's clap hands. (clap, clap, clap)

"You're doing so well," Dad says, "Let's keep going." He sings and the children again repeat each line.

There is so very much of me. Let's clap hands. (clap, clap, clap)

But you are you and I am me. Let's clap hands. (clap, clap, clap)

Whenever I sing my own song, I know for sure I can't go wrong.

All together let's sing this song. Let's clap hands. (clap, clap, clap)

The children were getting tired, but their parents hugged them and said, "Here's the end of the song. Just listen, and we'll learn the words another time. You can just hum along for now."

I may want to be a doctor. I clap hands. (clap, clap, clap)

You might want to be a teacher. Clap your hands. (clap, clap, clap)

I'll still be me, and you'll be you. We'll be us whatever we do.

All together let's sing this song. Let's clap hands. (clap, clap, clap)

Mom and Dad and Aunt Tu clap. Shadow barks. The children smile. Everybody is happy being together.

"Time to get ready for bed. You get started and I'll check on you in a few minutes," says Mom.

Donald and Linda wash, brush their teeth, and change into pajamas and surprise Mom when she comes into their bedrooms because they got ready so quickly.

Mom says to Linda in her room, "This book has a goodnight song, too. We can sing it to *Twinkle, Twinkle Little Star*, but it has different words. Tonight, I'll sing it to you. Tomorrow night I'll help you learn the words. There are other songs in this book for other days, and we'll get to them another time.

> *I love you just how you are.*
> *I love you both near and far.*
> *I love you both right and wrong.*
> *I love you and sing this song.*
> *I love you both wrong and right.*
> *I love you, so sleep. Good night! (They kiss and hug.)*

Mom goes to Donald's room and asks, "Would you like the song I sang to Linda?"

Donald is quiet and looks sad. "No, Mom. Not tonight.

If I were a girl, would you love me as much as you love Linda? She gets lots of hugs and kisses and Dad tickles her more than he does me."

Mom was quiet for a moment. "Donald," she said, "We love you very much. We love Linda very much, too, but we show that a little differently. We hug and kiss you a lot, too, but we love Linda differently because she's a girl. Dad plays rougher with you than he does with Linda. We want you both to grow up knowing that it's never O.K. for a boy to be rough with a girl. We love you both with a full heart, but just a little differently. Does that make sense?"

Now Donald was the one to be quiet. "Yes, I guess so," he said. "I never thought of it that way, but it does make sense. Girls play differently; they play with different stuff; they draw different kinds of pictures; they talk differently with their friends.

So, I guess it makes sense that their parents show their love for them differently."

"You're growing up, David".

"Girls can be good at stuff we're good at, like soccer and running fast. And boys can be good at stuff that girls are good at like singing and writing stories. But we really are different, so it makes sense that you and Dad show your love differently for each of us. But I like it when you say you love us each with a full heart. So, you love us the same after all!" Donald smiled and gave his mom a big hug for the full day and for love with a full heart.

Aunt Tu came into Donald's room to say good night, to tell him that she loved him very much, and that she was enjoying her visit. She'd be leaving right after his birthday and wouldn't be back for another two years, but she would write to them and send more books. She said she hoped they would grow up to be good readers because it opened ideas and the world for them.

Donald smiled and nodded off to sleep with a full heart.

Chapter Two – Happy Just the Way I Am

Donald is now seven years old, and Linda is five. Two years can make a big difference. You might want to re-read chapter one if you haven't read it for a long time so you can see the big difference in the way they think and talk to each other and their parents.

The doorbell rings at the Livengood's small brick house. Donald, Linda, and Shadow run to the front door because they are expecting their Aunt Tu, whom they haven't seen for two years.

"Hello Donald! Hello Linda! It's so good to see you, and how you've grown! And guess what?"

"You brought us a new book!" both the children exclaimed at the same time.

(Each chapter in the book you are holding was a separate small book for Donald and Linda. Aunt Tu was writing the books for them.)

"Yes, I have," said Aunt Tu. "I appreciate the 'thank you' note you sent me every time you received a book I sent you during my travels. Your notes helped me stay in touch with how you were doing, but now I can see just how much you have grown!"

"May I read this book with you?" asked Aunt Tu. It has songs in it, too, just like the other one. I like to sing, just like your mother and father.

"Yes, yes, Aunt Tu", said Linda. She really liked it when Aunt Tu read to them.

"I wrote a story that I would like to read to you," said Donald. He was very excited and tried very hard to sound grown-up.

"Well, then," said Aunt Tu, "I'd like to hear your story first, Donald. What's it about?"

He sat up very tall and explained.

"I have a friend at school. His name is Maximus. He says it means 'greatest', but he likes to be called Max. He can run very fast, but the other boys and some girls run faster because they are taller and have longer legs. Max is very short. Most people think he's in kindergarten instead of second grade. He doesn't like being so short. Kids call him "Maxie" in a sing-song voice. He hates it. He says he should have been a girl because everybody thinks short girls are cute. I thought about how I could make him feel better about being a short boy and wrote this story for him. He likes it.

Farmer Dell had a large garden with many tomato plants. He took such good care of them that his tomatoes were the largest and sweetest in the neighborhood. He gave a lot of them to the food bank and to neighbors, but he sold them at the farmers' market, too.

There was one tomato plant that was much smaller than all the others. He took it out of the garden and put it in a large pot and gave it to his wife to keep on the patio. She liked it because the leaves were a beautiful dark green and it had a lot of small yellow flowers.

The flowers became very small tomatoes. They grew and looked healthy, but they were much smaller than all the other tomatoes in Farmer Dell's garden. Ms. Dell waited until they were ripe, and then she picked them and put them on the dinner table in their own bowl with no other tomatoes on the table.

That night the family tasted the small tomatoes for the first time. What a surprise! They had a wonderful flavor! They were even sweeter than all the other tomatoes in the garden!

"These are perfect for taking to school in my lunch box," said their son, Maximum Max. They called him that because he

always tried so hard to be just as fast, just as tall, just as smart as the tallest, fastest, smartest students in the class.

"And I like them," said his mother, "because I can pick them from the patio, which is much closer than the garden."

"Hey," said Maximum Max, "even though they're the smallest, they're the best in their own way. I've always been like the small tomatoes. Maybe the short way that I am makes me the best in my own way!"

That's right, Max," said his father, Farmer Dell. Maybe you don't have to try so hard to be like everyone else. Maybe we can just call you Max, and all you have to do is your personal best. And we've always loved you just the way you are. You've always been special to us!"

"That's a wonderful story, Donald," said his Aunt Tu.

"And I'm special, too," said Linda. "I'm a girl and short and I like being just the way I am! And I wrote the song for this story! Well, Dad did help me. Do you want to hear it?"

"Definitely!" said Aunt Tu.

"OK. Here goes!" Donald and Linda sang this song to the tune of B-I-N-G-O.

There was a farmer had a son
And Maximus was his name!
MAXIMUS, MAXIMUS, MAXIMUS,
and Maximus was his name.

"What did your friend think of the story, Donald?" asked Aunt Tu.

He liked it so much he hums the tune all day long. Everybody thinks he's humming B-I-N-G-O. He likes keeping his real words secret, but when anybody teases him because he's so short, he looks them in the eye and says, 'I'm happy just the way I am.'"

Aunt Tu had to leave in just a few days. You may remember that she travels a lot for her job, even to other countries. But she remembers Donald's story and Linda's song as the best part of her visit.

Chapter Three – Growing While They're Learning

The Livengood children continued to become taller, faster, and smarter. Linda is now seven, in 2nd grade, and Donald is nine, in fourth grade. Aunt Tu's job has kept her at her company's home office in London, England for two years. She has stayed in touch with her niece and nephew but has missed them. She is looking forward to seeing them again during this visit. She is also very excited about her first meeting with Sam and Sue, the fraternal twins born after her last visit. (Fraternal twins are two children born to the same mother at the same time! They can be either two boys, two girls, or a boy and a girl. Identical twins are always either two girls or two boys.) Tomorrow is their second birthday.

Aunt Tu walks up to their door, rings the bell, and of course hears Shadow barking at the sound.

Donald sees his aunt through the window and eagerly lets her in.

"Donald," Aunt Tu says, giving him a big hug and kiss, "It's so good to see you again, but I'm used to seeing Linda with you when I open the door. Where is she?"

"She's helping Mom with Sam and Sue. She's *always* helping Mom with Sam and Sue! But I don't see you carrying a book for us this time", Donald said with clear disappointment.

"As you know, I've written the books I've brought you, but I've been so busy that I couldn't finish the one I'm writing for you. I hope to have it for my next visit, but I do have a song you can help me sing to your little brother and sister.

For the rest of the afternoon Aunt Tu was busy unpacking, visiting with the family, and helping to prepare dinner. She's a really good cook!

After Sam and Sue were sound asleep, they all sat in the living room and Aunt Tu taught Donald and Linda the new song, sung to the tune of *Happy Birthday*. They learned the words quickly and were ready to sing it when the little ones woke up in the morning. They sang together one more time:

> *Welcome birth-day to Sam,*
> *Welcome birth-day to Sue,*
> *Welcome birth-day dear children,*
> *You are our dream come true!*
> *A little boy are you,*
> *A little girl are you,*
> *We're so happy you're with us,*
> *You are our dream come true.*

"You know," Linda said, "Sam and Sue don't look exactly alike. And Sam is quiet, but Sue is talking almost all the time. They're really different in a lot of ways.

"They sure are," Mom said slowly, and you could see how tired she is. "Sue is all girl and Sam's boy-ness will be coming along soon, I'm sure."

"What's it mean, 'all girl?'" asked Linda.

"And what's 'boy-ness', and where is Sam's?" Donald wanted to know.

Mom seemed so weary, so Dad answered, "Mom means that Sue is a happy little chatterbox. Girls many times find their voice and words sooner than boys, and 'boy-ness' means a rough-and-tumble way of looking for adventure that little boys many times develop very young. But these are not always true for all girls and all boys. Little girls can be rough and tumble, too. Our friend's daughter has always been highly active and she's an excellent young gymnast. But either way, one thing's sure. Every cell in Sue's body is a girl cell and every cell in Sam's body is a boy cell."

Both children started asking questions all at once, "What's a cell? Do I have cells? What do cells do?"

"Whoa! Just a minute. One question at a time," Dad said, laughing. "All the parts of you are made up of smaller and smaller parts. Like your arm has a shoulder, elbow, wrist, hand, and fingers, and all of those have many small bones, yes?"

The children smiled and nodded.

"The smallest parts of every part of your body are cells, too small to see."

Eye cells help you see. Brain cells work with arm cells and finger cells to help you pick up things. Your body has trillions of cells. A trillion is way more than hundreds, thousands, millions, and billions. And every one of your cells is a boy cell or girl cell. You will grow and change in many, many ways, but your cells will always stay *you*!"

"So, is that what it means to say that Sue is 'all girl'?" asked Linday.

"Well, yes," Dad answered, "but much more than that. It also means that although girls can do just about everything that boys can do…"

"And better, too!" Linda interrupted.

"That can be true," said Dad. "But girls also have some ways of seeing and thinking and feeling that are different from boys. We always say that you and Donald are the greatest gifts to us, and your ways as Linda-girl are gifts to us and to other people, too."

"So, I'm guessing this has something to do with Sam's boy-ness, and mine, too," said Donald, who was looking very thoughtful. "But I love to sing and to write and I get teased at school because kids say, 'that's girl stuff'. So, it's confusing."

"Donald," Dad said slowly. "You and your friends will find that there is no end to the "stuff" you can learn. Shadow is a very smart dog, and she is looking and learning all the time, isn't she? But she can only learn and do so much because she's a dog. There's almost no limit to what people can learn and think and do, so it's not ever fair to say, 'she's just a girl', or 'he's just a boy'. And it does limit everyone when someone says, 'music is for girls', or 'baseball is for boys'.

You and Linda are very different, and some of that difference is because you are a boy, and she is a girl. What's most important is that you both learn to love with a full heart, your very own heart, just the way you are."

"This is a lot to think about," said Mom. Now I have a new song for you before you go to bed." She didn't look so tired when she said that.

"Do you remember, 'She'll be coming 'round the mountain when she comes'?", Mom asked.

Both children smiled and nodded 'yes'!

"Let's use the music from that song for these words. I'll sing it first and you can join in when you're ready."

They'll be learning while they're growing; yes they will.
They'll be learning while they're growing; yes they will.
They'll be learning while they're growing;
They'll be learning while they're growing;
They'll be learning while they're growing;
yes they will!
They'll be growing while they're learning; yes they will.
They'll be growing while they're learning; yes they will.
They'll be growing while they're learning;
They'll be growing while they're learning;
They'll be growing while they're learning;

yes they will!

"Now give us a hug and kiss…"
"With a full heart," both Donald and Linda chimed in, as they scrambled to get to their parents and Aunt.
"… and go get ready for bed," Mom finished, with a sigh.
Can you guess what Linda and Donald were humming as they got ready for bed?

Chapter Four – I Have Dignity

Linda and Donald Livengood have been learning while they're growing and growing while they're learning. Donald is now 11, in sixth grade, and Linda is now nine, in fourth grade. The twins, Sam and Sue, are four. Their beloved Aunt Tu has always visited them every other year because her job keeps her far away. This time she comes in time for the twins' birthday and brings presents for all four of them, a children's book that she has written. She has come a few days before the birthday party because she wants to talk to Mr. and Ms. Livengood about Sam, whom she hasn't seen since he was two. This is the first night of her visit.

"Thank you for keeping me up to date about Sam's progress with his special services," Aunt Tu says to Sam's parents as they talk in the living room after all the children are asleep. "It's been a big concern of mine, too, that he still isn't talking."

Ms. Livengood begins to fill in Sam's history with some information she hasn't shared by phone or e-mail.

"Even in person, it's still hard to describe just how different Sam is. We've told you how interested in music Sam is. He hums everything he listens to. And he swirls and dances to music for a very long time. He isn't the fastest kid in his pre-school class, but when they all go out to recess, he runs all the way to the back fence and then runs around the playground until he can't run any more. We've told you how he loves books but wait until you see his concentration as he looks at them. He acts like he's reading, points across the words in each line, smiles, laughs, and seems to understand the story, even if it's one we haven't read to him for quite a while. His memory is amazing."

Sam's father adds, "Sam is usually a good-natured boy, but he can be demanding. We set clear limits, but if Sam doesn't want to do something, he doesn't. A few days ago, we called him in for dinner. He shook his head and stayed outside to look at baby birds in a nest. He didn't come in until we finished eating, until it was starting to get dark."

"And he never even tries to say words?" asked Aunt Tu.

"Sue is forever talking for him," says Ms. Livengood. "Sam has a very expressive face and gestures and hand signals, which Sue understands. She tries to let us know what he's thinking and what he wants."

"And Sam corrects her, if need be," laughs Sam's father. "Sue understands Sam without even trying and sometimes can bring him what he wants or needs even before he tries to communicate it. She's very intuitive and protective, although Sam is so much stronger than she is.

And he is very, very interested in machines and trucks, the bigger the better. Every time we see a big truck; he gets so excited he can't sit still. He starts humming and waving his hands and pointing to show us the big truck."

"The one we're starting to worry about now," says Mom, "is Donald. Some of the neighborhood kids tell him his brother is dumb. The first time Donald yelled back, 'He is not. He just can't talk.' One of the boys told him, 'That's what dumb means – can't talk'. That's been hard on Donald. He's very angry and even gets mad at Sam and at us."

"Sam doesn't seem to mind though," his mother puts in. "Sam has a very strong sense of his own dignity. Tomorrow, I think you'll see what I mean. Notice the way he sits and walks and looks at people, especially when they talk to him. He seems to say, 'I am me, and that's alright.' I wrote a song to help Donald and Linda understand the dignity Sam shows, and to better understand their own. I've been trying to decide the right time to teach it to them."

They talked into the night, for there was much to learn about the last two years in each other's lives, and much to consider about the children.

The next morning at breakfast Aunt Tu observed Sam closely without showing it. Sam observed her, but it was quite noticeable. He looked at every move she made, listened to every word, and took in every expression on her face and gesture of her hands. And Mom noticed Donald observing them.

It was a windy, rainy Saturday. After cleaning up and chores, Sam played with his big blocks next to Donald who was working on a LEGO kit. Linda and Sue went to their dance classes. Later, while Sam took a nap, Donald worked on his project about stars for his science class. Ever since he was a little boy, he has been interested in the stars and other planets. When the family went camping a few years ago and Donald saw the night sky from the dark mountains, he was more than interested – he was amazed. Then he really began to study them. Linda caught his enthusiasm. Her genuine interest and serious study led her to be the "expert" among the students in her class.

That night, after dinner, Mom decided the time might be right to try to teach the children her song to help them learn about their dignity. Donald needed strength to face the teasing about his brother, and the other girls in Linda's dance class were putting her down for being "different" because she didn't like their gossip. Mom called them together while Aunt Tu played with Sam and Sue in the next room.

"Donald and Linda," Mom began, "I know how tough teasing can be. Dad and I faced our share when we were growing up, and even as adults sometimes. It can hurt. I want you to know about the dignity you have by just being you, and to protect that dignity from anybody who makes fun of you. Dignity means that you are special and important just being yourself. Donald and Sam were born to be our sons. Linda and Sue were born to be our daughters. It is your birthright to have dignity in that. Other kids have to learn to respect you for who you are. Even when they don't, Dad and I want you to keep your dignity at all times. It means believing in yourself, even if it feels like nobody else does, because we always believe in you, even if we sometimes don't like something you say or do.
You can keep your dignity in a quiet way. Never call names or put anyone down. They must keep their dignity, too,

because everyone is important and special, even if sometimes they forget it.

You remember the song, *Oh, When the Saints Go Marchin' In*. We're going to sing these words to that music. Dad and I will sing it first, like we always do. Here's a copy of the words so you can follow along. Just hum the first time, and then we'll sing it together.

Oh yes, you mean so much to me,
Oh yes, you mean so much to me,
I want you always to remember,
that you mean so much to me.
From the moment, you were alive,
From the moment, you were alive,
You were more than all the stars,
From the moment, you were alive.
Please hold yourself so tall and strong,
Please hold yourself so tall and strong,
Always believe in your dignity,
Hold yourself so tall and strong.
Yes, you are you, and no one else,
Yes, you are you, and no one else,
Worth more than stars is your dignity,
You are you, and no one else.

Donald was all smiles, but Linda had a puzzled look on her face. "Where is my dignity," she asked. How do I find it? How do I keep it?"

"Very important questions, Linda," said Dad, looking pleased. "Dignity comes from knowing that you are loved, that you are the only you in the world, that you have a purpose for your life."

"I know you and Mom and Donald and Sue and Sam and Aunt Tu and Shadow love me," smiled Linda, but sometimes being the only me is a lonely feeling because I'm different from the other girls." Now she wasn't smiling.

"That's what it means to be unique, just yourself, different from everyone else," said Mom. "Yes, it can be a lonely feeling, for sure, and that's why so many people try so hard to fit in, so they won't feel lonely. But lonely doesn't mean that you are alone. We are with you, in your full heart, even when we're not with you. Always remember God loves you and is always with you; we've taught you that. And when you think of all that you know and still want to learn, all that you can do, all that you like and don't like, the places you've been and want to go, your desire to be a dancer when you grow up, then you have yourself and *your* life for company, too. Being unique can then start to feel special, because there's no one else exactly like you. We want you to honor that, to know that you are worth more than all the stars to us. You are trustworthy because we believe in you, even when we let each other down sometimes. Your worth as a human being, as our daughter, as our one-and-only Linda, gives you a dignity that you must know and believe and trust and realize that no one and nothing can ever take that from you, no matter what."

Linda had tears in her eyes. "That's a lot to think about, Mom. I'm only nine years old. I don't know that I understand all that, completely, but I guess I can grow into it. I think that when I'm feeling down, I'll sing this song." Linda looked at the words. Everyone was quiet. "I really like the ending, but when I sing it I could change it this way."

Yes, I am me, and no one else,
Yes, I am me, and no one else,
Worth more than the stars is my dignity,
I am me, and no one else.

Linda started marching and dancing and singing these words. Soon she was spinning and leaping with a look of great concentration and pride. "*I am me, and no one else.*" Her smile was glowing. "I have dignity!"

Aunt Tu, Sam and Sue had come into the room just in time to see Linda singing and dancing. Sue started spinning around and around. Sam watched, a curious smile on his face. When Linda sat down and all the family were smiling, Mom with tears in her eyes, Sam said, "Dignity. Me, too."

Everyone stopped breathing. "Sam, you talked!!" Mom's tears were a waterfall down her cheeks. She went to Sam and took both his hands in hers and looked into his eyes.

"Mom, don't cry," he said.

She started laughing and gave him a big, big hug. So did Aunt Tue. Everyone rushed to hug Sam.

Dad always had words for everything. Now it was Dad's turn to be speechless.

Chapter Five – What a Team!

"Dad, I have a really big problem," Donald confided as they went for a walk, just the two of them. It was the beginning of 8th grade and Donald was 13. "My friend Max has changed a lot over the summer. He says he wants to be a girl. I tried to shrug it off. I told him it's because he's the shortest in the class. I reminded him that ever since second grade he's been thinking he should have been a girl because he's so short and everybody thinks short girls are cute. He said he doesn't even feel like a boy. He even *feels* like a girl, he says. He wants to run on the girl's track team because he thinks he can win and that way everyone will respect him and not tease him anymore. He hangs out with the girls and says they think he's funny. They don't tease him. He says he fits in with the girls, but not the boys. He says his parents are pretty upset. Max's been my friend my whole life, it seems. What should I do?"

They stopped walking and sat on a bench in the shade by the pond, underneath a large cottonwood tree. Dad was quiet. Donald waited.

"First thing," Dad said, "is to keep being his friend. True friends don't give up on each other. It may be just a phase he's going through. He may outgrow it, even if he doesn't get much taller." Dad smiled at his play-on-words, but when he looked at Donald, he stopped smiling.

"I don't think so, Dad. He's even started wearing make-up."

Again, Dad was quiet a while before he spoke. "Did you ever hear the word "transgender", Donald?", he asked.

"Yes, I think it's where somebody changes their sex. Kids talk about it."

"Well," said Dad, "the first thing to understand that although someone can change appearances, behaviors, and even physical features, it's impossible to actually change one's sex. I know it's been years, but when Sam and Sue were just two years old, we talked about how different they were, about their boy-ness and girl-ness. Do you remember?

Donald wrinkled his forehead trying to remember and finally nodded yes.

"At that time, I said 'Your body has trillions of cells. And every one of your cells is a boy cell or girl cell. You will grow and change in many ways, but your cells will always stay you, starting with the way you were when you were born!' Maybe teachers haven't told you that, but it's true. I have a couple of articles from trusted sources that I'll read with you that explain this in more detail.

I've had transgender students in my classes. They've always appreciated that I've treated them with respect and just like all the other students. They've been intelligent and capable. They've done their best and produced good work. And I've done my best to help them develop their skills, just like I try my best for all my students.

But it's an error to think that someone can actually change his or her sex, his or her gender, which is a gift we're born with and part of our nature, a very important part of who we are as human beings."

"But Dad," Donald replied, "Max has talked with his doctor and has done a lot of reading and says that it is possible to have a sex change, and he wants to do it."

"Donald," Dad explains, "it is possible to change many physical features, but it's not possible to cancel one's birthright to be male or female. A person who has fully transitioned in appearance from male to female, or the other way around, has to stay on cross-sex hormones for the rest of his or her life to override a true birth-nature. And there can be much harm done."

"Now I'm really worried," says Donald, "and there's more, too. The same kids that used to tease me when Sam couldn't talk now tease me for being Max's friend. Max seems to keep his dignity through it all and handle it OK, but I don't. I lay awake thinking about it and get confused and don't know what to do. I'm losing some of the friends I've had a long time, and there's a girl I really like, but I'm not sure what she thinks."

"Donald," Dad replies, "anyone who teases or insults you does not understand dignity, yours or theirs or anyone's. Some people think that you have to earn dignity in some way, with accomplishment, money, or popularity. That's not true. Dignity is a God-given right for everyone. Our Declaration of Independence, constitution, and Bill of Rights support that, and your parents certainly do, too. Maybe you could share these thoughts with the girl you like. Maybe she'd understand. Maybe it would help your friendship with her grow because it's about something important to you."

"Dad, all due respect, but that doesn't help me in the hallways, cafeteria, on the playground, or going back and forth to school. Kids can be cruel. How do I manage that? And how do I help Max? He gets teased much, much worse than I do. And even bullied. It's bound to get to him sooner or later."

"Donald, it might help a little to know that everyone in all times and places has had to face bullies, or even worse, persecution for who they are or what they believe. The beginning of your inner strength comes from knowing yourself, knowing right from wrong, and being in touch with *your* dignity. Think about that for a while.

You've been getting pretty good with your guitar, and I know you enjoy writing songs as much as I do. It's a great way to work out ideas, feelings, and experiences. Why not give that a try? Singing one of your own songs to yourself when times are tough can really give you a lift."

Donald looked thoughtful for a few minutes, then said, "Thanks Dad. Talking with you has really helped. I think I would like to talk to Celia about all this. I've been afraid to, but I'm not now. If you don't mind. I'd like to sit here by myself for a while before I go home."

Dad certainly did not mind. Donald always carried some note cards and a pencil. He could compose a song much faster writing than he could on his cell phone. After a few drafts and much revision, he came up with something he liked, to the tune of *This Land Is Your Land*.

When he got home, he showed Dad, who hummed the tune as he read it.

"Donald, this is really good. I'm impressed! I have a couple of suggestions you might consider. Here, how does this sound? And here, would this wording help?"

His son looked at the changes, smiled, and said, "Yes, definitely. I like this better."

Together they sang:

To be free and equal, we are created,
to give love and kindness, and not be hated
as we search our right path and try to take it,
dignity belongs to you and me.

"What a team!" Dad exclaimed.

Donald's broad smile told him that he definitely agreed.

Donald caught up with Max on his way home from school. He was excited to share his song and let him know that, no matter what, he was still his friend. But when he looked at the expression on Max's face, he lost the song somewhere deep inside.

Max said, "We're moving. Mom said she knows a better school for me, where I won't be teased. Where I'll fit in better and have friends. Donald, you're the only friend I have left. None of the boys will even talk to me, except to make fun of me, and even the girls don't want to be my friend anymore. They said they're afraid the boys won't like them.

If it's OK with you, I'll stay in touch and let you know how I'm doing."

Donald handed him a copy of his song that he had illustrated. "Maximus, you're the greatest.

I want to give this to you. I wrote it for me and for you, with my dad's help." Max looked so downcast that Donald didn't know what to do or say, so he just clapped him on the shoulder, the way they always used to do, and turned away. He walked home very slowly.

Chapter Six – Peaceful

"Mom," said Linda, her 13-year-old daughter. "Can we have a talk?" Whenever Linda used that tone of voice, Ms. Livengood knew there was something serious coming.

"Sure. Let's go out back and sit in the shade."

"Mom, I'm worried about Donald. Just because he's 15 and in high school, he doesn't ever talk to me anymore, about anything important, I mean. Yesterday I saw him kiss Celia at the park, and last night as I walked past his bedroom, I heard him say on the phone, 'I like it that you call me Dignus when we're alone'."

"Now, a kiss and a pet nickname – that does sound serious," Mom said in a light voice with her eyebrows raised.

"Mom, I'm serious. Donald doesn't even talk about Max anymore. They used to talk on the phone a lot after Max moved to his new school, and Donald used to talk about it with me since I was good friends with Max, too. He told me how very lonely

Max was, how different he feels, how he still can't seem to fit in anywhere, even though there are transgender kids at the school, and they're accepted, mostly. Donald tried to encourage him, but Max is so far down in the dumps that even Donald can't cheer him up. Slowly they started drifting apart. And now all Donald thinks about is his schoolwork, his music, and Celia. I hear him in his room practicing songs for her, to her, about her.

Ever since he's been racing that fancy bike he

bought with all the money he's saved through the years, he seems to think it's beneath him to go cycling with me. And every chance he gets he rides to Celia's house, an hour away. I know he wears a helmet and takes bike paths to stay off the streets, but it seems like a long way for someone his age, doesn't it?"

Without waiting for an answer, she plunged into her next concern.

"And then there's this girl in my class. I don't want to tell you her name, but she's got me worried, too. I'm her only friend. She says the girls call her 'Plain Jane' because she never dresses fancy or wears make-up or gossips about boys. But what really worries me is now she's convinced that if she had a boyfriend, all her troubles would be over. She wouldn't be lonely anymore and the other girls would respect her. She's changing, fast. She's starting to flirt with the boys but she's awkward and self-conscious and gets teased more than ever. Kids are starting to say awful things about her, really awful comments and jokes, insulting her dignity as Donald would say."

"Linda," Mom said slowly, when she could get a word in. "First of all, about Donald, let's give him some time and respect his privacy. As you know, Dad and I and Donald have had lunch with Celia and her parents more than once. Donald and Celia are both trustworthy, and with his concern for the dignity of everybody, and from all I've observed, I'd say he'll honor Celia with his behavior.

I'm glad you're concerned about your brother's safety on his bike, but we've watched him race and he handles a bike very well. He doesn't risk his own safety or anyone else's.

Now as for your friend, I agree there are some worry-signs there. Why don't you invite her over? I'd like to meet her. And if it's OK with you, I'd like her to meet Donald."

After a long pause, Linda said, "I think that's a good idea, Mom. How about next Saturday? I'll tell her you bake the very best chocolate chip cookies. She loves them. And" Linda paused again, "I think it's a good idea for her to meet Donald. He really knows how to show respect. That will be very important for

Phoebe. Could we go to the lake? We could rent kayaks. Phoebe is a really strong swimmer."

The week passed quickly. Mom and Linda had explained the situation to Donald, and he understood so well that he said he'd like to invite Celia.

Saturday came to them at the lake with warm sunshine, a cool breeze, and the scent of wildflowers. They swam, went kayaking until their arms ached, and ate their fill of picnic lunch that offered more chocolate chip cookies than even hungry teenagers could finish. Everyone enjoyed seeing Sam and Sue, the eight-year-old twins, playing in the water. Sam seemed to have more energy than anyone. He was friendly and happy but also enjoyed looking at every little thing through his magnifying glass, 'collecting specimens' as he called it, and sitting by himself writing and drawing. Phoebe especially noticed that Sue kept a close eye on Sam and checked in with him often. She also noticed that both Sam and Sue observed her carefully, too, but with the smiles that made her feel accepted.

Mom and Dad went for a long walk, hand-in-hand, which Phoebe noticed. She said, "Your mom and dad still hold hands! And they help each other with everything. You both talk to them in such an open way. And Celia," she paused, and the others thought she might be holding back tears, "you're so accepted."

Nobody said anything, but the silence was not uncomfortable.

"I feel peaceful for the first time in a very long while," Phoebe said. "And I have a lot to think about."

"Phoebe," Celia said. "A special interest of mine is words, their meanings, their history. I looked up your name. Phoebe means bright, radiant, pure. It's also a type of songbird."

No one spoke. Finally, Phoebe said, through tears, "Yes, I sure do have a lot to think about."

Chapter Seven – The Gift of a Full Heart

"A great leader of one of the world's largest religions believes that recognizing human dignity is a fundamental condition for our societies to be truly just, peaceful, healthy, and authentically human. I wish that all activists for any issue would think about that, Aunt Tu."

Aunt Tu had finally taken a long-needed vacation and come to stay with the Livengoods for a full week. She enjoyed listening to her 17-year-old nephew, Donald. They had been talking for over an hour about all the difficult and complicated situations in the country and in the world: poverty, war, the treatment of migrants, human trafficking, sexual abuse. She was also impressed with her 15-year-old niece, Linda, who had sat through the entire conversation, offering a comment now and then or asking a question.

Now Linda piped up, "I'll tell you what all the activists should get united about: violence toward women. Your 'great leader' calls it a scandal and that women aren't seen as having the same dignity as men. Therefore," and now Linda was sitting up as tall as she could be, "there is no true equality! What do you have to say about that, Dignus?"

They all used Celia's nickname for Donald only on special occasions. This conversation was the deepest, strongest, and longest they've had for quite a while. Leave it to Aunt Tu to bring out the best in everyone.

Donald answered, "You're right, Little Sister." That surprised her so much she didn't know what to say next.

Phoebe had been invited overnight and was listening avidly to every word but hadn't yet spoken.

"I think," Phoebe cleared her throat. Everyone looked at her, surprised but smiling. "I think," she repeated, "that along with all the forms of violence against women that are so widely known, there's another: uncaring silence about their suffering, cold silence toward them when they want to be accepted and understood, bored silence with them when they want to share their thoughts and feelings in an open way, and distant silence about the true love they need. These are also forms of violence toward women – the violence of silence."

Everyone was stunned. They had no idea how strong and eloquent Phoebe could be. But Max was not surprised at all. He had been invited as a special guest. After a long absence from their lives, he had called Donald and asked to come for a visit. He remembered Aunt Tu from his early childhood and had always trusted her, and of course had a special love for the Livengoods as the only other family besides his own that had always accepted him and cared about him.

Everyone noticed how good he looked. He had cut his hair, gained muscle and maturity, and seemed older but with a sense of sadness.

Max said, "Phoebe is right." This was another surprise, although Linda had sensed that there was a relationship between the two of them, even though she had never seen them together.

"We met last summer and have become good friends. She's been honest with me about her troubles, and I've told her things I haven't told anyone else. 'Til now.

I ran away from home and lived on the streets for about a month. I met some good people, but a lot of bad ones. It was much more loneliness than I ever felt. I finally went home and told my parents how sorry I was for what I put them through. They hugged me, cried a lot, forgave me, and kept saying how glad they were that I was home.

I learned a lot about song writing from David, and wrote this one, along with plenty of others. It takes after *St. Louis Blues*, a very old song, and uses that melody. The title comes from thoughts Phoebe shared with me, and just now with you. But the experiences are mine. Donald, may I borrow your guitar?"

Silence Violence

Oh, my friends don't want to see me around.
Oh no, they don't want to see me around.
teas'n isn't pleas'n for me nohow.
Silence hurts big when no one says your name.
It wrenches deep when no one says your name.
Feelin' lonely finds each day just the same.
Silence is a violence of deep alone.
It leaves you out with freezin' to your bones.
Silence violence feels like you have no home.
It feels like you have no home.

The only one who wasn't surprised was Phoebe, who took Max's hand.

"I sang this, and other songs for Phoebe, and it's because of her encouragement that I'm here and could sing for you. She knows a lot about my past and still accepts me for who I am. That's more than I can do. Donald, I know that dignity has always been very important to you. Now you know someone who doesn't have any. I've done some shameful things.

But I am trying to turn my life around. I've been lifting weights and running a lot. I've got a good part-time job while I'm back in school. I'm involved with two of what are called 'internal martial arts'. They work a lot by controlling an opponent's balance rather than punching and kicking. Their philosophy appeals to me. And I go out of my way to step up to any situation where someone is being bullied. I'm keeping a daily journal and being as honest as I can be with myself. Slowly I'm earning back the right to have some dignity."

Everyone was quiet, in a very respectful and caring way.

"Thank you for listening. I feel relieved and ... proud of myself. It's a great feeling. Thank you!"

Phoebe had tears in her eyes, as did Linda. Aunt Tu was smiling. Donald looked very serious. He was the first to speak.

"Max, it's so good to have you back. Thank *you* for being so honest and straightforward with us. You've certainly earned my respect. But if I may, I'd like to clear up a common confusion about dignity that can hopefully make you feel a lot better about yourself.

There are different kinds of dignity. Any of us can lose our moral dignity by making bad choices, but as you are doing, it's possible to regain that kind of dignity.

There's dignity in a way of life, by living in a very healthy way; for example, by living with joy and hope and care for oneself and others.

There's dignity or lack of dignity in the conditions in which we live. For example, when people are living in extreme poverty through no fault of their own and struggle greatly just to survive, there's no fairness or dignity in that.

All of these forms of dignity may be lost or gained, earned or given up or taken away by others or by circumstances.

The most important dignity we'll call *being* dignity. It belongs to you the moment you come to be and doesn't end. It's not given and can't be given up or taken away. It's just because you are you, a one-and-only you, a human being. There may be life on other planets in other solar systems, even intelligent life as we might discover someday, but as far as we know for sure, human beings are unique, and each one of us is unique, and that inherits and deserves a very special dignity. So even if someone loses any or all of the other forms of dignity, he or she can never lose the dignity that comes with being a human being."

Again, everyone was quiet, thinking, understanding, believing, accepting what Donald said. It was easy to see in him his father the teacher, his mother the clear and caring one, his aunt who took any opportunity to make a difference.

Finally, it was Linda who spoke first.

"Donald, years ago, when you and I were especially interested in the stars and other planets, Mom and Dad made up a song to help us understand dignity. I didn't understand it, and asked a lot of questions. They explained and it helped, but it really helped for me to sing the song over and over until I felt I understood dignity much better, although not nearly as much as I do now. Do you remember? Could we sing it again? Max and Phoebe might like to hear it."

Max and Phoebe were smiling to show that yes, they would like that.

Donald held out his hand and Max gave him the guitar. Donald said, "Yes, I do remember it. It got me started on what I suppose will be a life-long quest to understand dignity, to live it, to support it in others. It goes to the tune of *Oh, When the Saints Go Marchin' In*."

Oh yes, you mean so much to me,
Oh yes, you mean so much to me,
I want you always to remember,
that you mean so much to me.
From the moment, you were alive,
From the moment, you were alive,
You were more than all the stars,
From the moment, you were alive.
Please hold yourself so tall and strong,
Please hold yourself so tall and strong,
Always believe in your dignity,
Hold yourself so tall and strong.
Yes, you are you, and no one else,
Yes, you are you, and no one else,
Worth more than stars is your dignity,
You are you, and no one else.

Part way through Linda did something she had never even thought about doing before. She was so happy and excited that she jumped up and started dancing. Everyone started clapping to the beat.

When Donald stopped playing, Linda said, "And do you remember that after the song I said how much I liked it and that I could change the ending to this, and she sang:"

Yes, I am me, and no one else,
Yes, I am me, and no one else,
Worth more than the stars is my dignity,
I am me, and no one else.

Max quickly took up the song for himself, in his much deeper voice,

Yes, I am me, and no one else,
Yes, I am me, and no one else,
Worth more than my faults is my dignity,
I am me, and no one else.

With that everyone stood up and rushed to hug him.

The rest of the evening was spent in friendly conversation. Aunt Tu brought a platter of Ms. Livengood's very large chocolate chip cookies and a large bowl of home-made vanilla ice cream, especially made for this occasion. Then she quietly said her goodbyes and left the 'young people' as she called them. Donald excused himself to finish an assignment for school.

Linda said to Phoebe and Max, "We have an expression in our family: *a full heart*. It goes back as far as I can remember. I share that with you now because that's how I feel, being here with you -- with a full heart".

Phoebe said, "Linda, your friendship has made a difference in my life, and I'm grateful. You and your family have accepted me, have taught me the meaning of genuine acceptance.

It's a rare and beautiful thing, and it is helping me grow into the person I want to be, the person I was meant to be."

Max added, "I feel like a stronger person than when I came in the door. We have memories together that go back to early in our childhoods. Tonight is a solid rock for me to build on. You all have given me a full heart!"

Chapter Eight – Good Company

The Livengood Family had grown in an unexpected way. Linda, now 17, had become best friends with Phoebe, also 17. They both were close to Donald's girlfriend Celia, 19, who spent time with them when she was home from college. Sam and Sue, the fraternal twins, now 12, felt that they had more than two sisters since the other girls were at the house so much, and Phoebe even went on summer vacation with them sometimes. Sue loved the attention from the other girls and could give a good imitation of each, to everyone's great laughter.

Sam was so busy with school, his "independent research projects", and being a patrol leader in his scout troop that he didn't have time for "socializing", as he called it.

An important part of the young ladies' time together was standing on the sidewalk by a local abortion clinic with signs that said *Choose Life*. They had many stories of the appreciation they received from passers-by as well as obscenities and aggressiveness from others.

Once, when the topic of abortion came up, Donald mentioned, without trying to sound like a know-it-all, that just three years after it was formed the United Nations issued a declaration which speaks about "the *inherent* dignity and of the equal and inalienable rights of all members of the human family." He and Celia wrote many letters to the editor. Of the many poems she wrote, this was one she really liked.

Too Quiet to See

It's easy to see
the power in storms,
in the rampant unfurled,
upheavals, even in
acceptable norms
for deciding and abiding all manner of things.
What do we see in the eye of the mind
for the growth and striving of life in the womb,
in the oft doubted urging of each living cell
that together adventure and unfold to be born?
Can we, dare we even believe?
in the strength of a beginning too quiet to see?

Linda and Phoebe, and Celia when she could, attended legislative sessions for pro-life bills in the senate and House of Representatives in their state. They thought of themselves as "pro-life partners".

Max was sympathetic, but working long hours in his father's shop and going to trade school as well kept him from joining in their many activities. They hadn't spent any time together for the past couple of years, but stayed in touch however, and on a recent phone call he asked to come over to meet with them all again.

A clear, peaceful Friday evening found them all gathered in the backyard of the Livengoods, Max with his guitar.

"The last time we were all together, I sang a very gloomy song about an especially sad chapter of my life," he said, but he sounded rather upbeat. "This time I'd like to sing something very different for you, something I've been working on in spare moments since we were all together. It's to a tune I think you all know: *I've Been Working on the Railroad*. It's called *Gratitude and Blessing*:

He began with a smile in a strong, clear voice.

I've been doin' lots of thinkin' all the live-long day
there's so much to be grateful for, worries melt away
Can't you see the difference in me, I rise so early in the morn
Gratitude is the song for me, bless when I was born!
Friends please sing with me, friends please sing with me.
Please rise up and sing this song, this song
Friends please sing with me, friends please sing with me
Please rise up and sing this song.
You share your love and light in my life
I'm better because of who you are
You share your love and light in my life
I thank you with my guitar
A-singin here and there and everywhere
Singin' altogether or if I'm far
Even if I'm livin' far
I'll be singin' with my guitar!

Happy clapping filled the air as a full moon began to rise above the trees.

They were all listening to Max eagerly.

"I needed to take a good, long and hard look at myself. Who am I, really? What's most important to me? Of all the many desires, hopes, and fears that churn inside me, which ones really do belong to me? Which ones do I want to be part of who I am? There's an old story about a Cherokee young man who spoke this way to the wisest person he knew: "Grandfather, I feel like I have two large, strong wolves fighting within me. One is very good. One is very bad. Which one will win?" His grandfather quietly replied, "Whichever one you feed, my son". That's how I've felt a lot, and that's why I like to call you all my friends and try to keep to the lifelong path of true dignity I've seen with you. It feeds my good wolf."

Phoebe was smiling proudly. She and Max were now holding hands.

Linda said, "Max, we've learned from you that it is possible to go through dark times and come back into the light. We are so happy for you and for Phoebe, for we've seen how strong and healthy she's become, too." Phoebe blushed at the attention, and you could see how glad she felt at the comment.

Celia quickly joined in. "Max, it's not all been easy for Donald and for me, either. Each of us has been troubled about what we should study and what we should do with our lives. We've changed our minds more than once, each time with painful soul searching. Under the pressure we haven't been our best for each other and we've broken up twice, painfully each time. Confusion and uncertainty are uncomfortable for anyone."

Then Donald spoke. "As I imagine how you all see me, how other people see me, I suppose it appears that I'm always sure of myself. No one sees me in the middle of the night when I can't sleep and have to face alone the many doubts about myself, what I believe, what I truly want and want to be. Celia has helped me more than I can say, but there's always that time alone when each of us has to face our weaknesses, temptations, and failures. So Max, you're in good company with us in many ways. And that includes the friendship and trust and happiness we feel together that we all need, that -- if I may say so -- support our dignity! "

Everyone laughed with appreciation and gratitude for Donald's honesty. Any thoughts about his lack of humility were laid to rest.

The friends were able to spend a lot of time together in the next few weeks. Donald and Celia were on a two-week break from college that coincided with one at Linda's and Phoebe's high school. Max's trade school was also closed for a short vacation and his father gave him time off from the shop. Their friendship continued to deepen during mountain hikes and picnics, swimming, canoeing and kayaking on the lake, and late nights by a campfire. There was no more need for soul-searching for a while, just lots of singing, laughing, and fun.

Chapter Nine – Look Deep Within

Mr. and Ms. Livengood have celebrated their 25th wedding anniversary and Mr. Livengood has turned 50. He still runs three days a week, swims, and rides his bike in age-group races as well as on all the local bike paths. He recently signed up for a "century", a 100-mile bike race, though as he says, "I'm not racing, just riding, though as fast as I can", and he laughs. Ms. Livengood has just published her first book, a book for young children learning to read. Aunt Tu has moved back to the U.S., much closer to the Livengoods, and in her retirement is finding much more time to be with them. She's especially attached to 14-year-old Sue and fully supports her dream to be a nurse aboard the USNS Mercy, a hospital ship that travels around the world to provide medical attention to people who rarely see a doctor.

Twin brother Sam, too, wants to be on the water, in a naval research vessel. He's planning to join the NROTC to give him a head start. In the meantime, as he says, "Eating, sleeping, and research – three primary needs of man." He still finds time for scouts and is working on his Eagle badge, which of course involves considerable research.

Linda joined a dance group straight out of high school, though her parents wanted her to continue with higher education first. "Mom, Dad," she said. "I'm young, healthy, a good dancer, and want to go places and see things. Another year and I'll settle down to four more years of studying, but not yet *please*!"

Her good friend Phoebe wants to be a counselor and is an inspiration for Sue because she is so focused and diligent. She'll be starting school when she returns from two years with the Peace Corps. As she says to the Livengoods," You helped me make something of my life; it's my turn to help people who desperately need help, as I did".

Max says he'll wait for Phoebe to return. He has so much to do before he can provide for her and a family. He's finished trade school and working full time as a partner in his father's business. His father is moving slowly to retirement while gradually turning over more and more responsibility to his son. Max is taking management and leadership classes at night because he has clear ambitions for expansion to a second site, but wants a good grounding in some advanced business fundamentals. Phoebe stands by him firmly and helps however she can. They make a strong team.

Donald and Celia are planning to get married, no surprise I'm sure, dear reader, but first they have some groundwork to do. They're about to graduate, he in journalism and she in political philosophy. Donald is currently interviewing for a start to his career and Celia is volunteering at a pregnancy resource center as they wait to see where they might have to relocate. "I'm confident I can get a good job anywhere," Celia says. No doubt she can. And again, it will come as no surprise that at a recent high school reunion Donald and Celia were voted "Most Dignified Couple"!

I talked with each of the family and friends individually at the anniversary celebration and found them all to be humble people, fully aware of their weaknesses, struggles, and failures. I mentioned this to Celia, who had been having a long talk with Mr. Livengood, and she said, "Yes, humility, having a modest view of oneself. Humus, Latin for earth and a root of the word humility, also of the word human. I think we're supposed to be down-to-earth, not to pump ourselves up to be more than we really are. It always helps to take a good look inside to find our true identity, to answer the question: Who am I, really?"

At the end of the celebration everyone formed a semi-circle around the celebrated couple, Mr. and Ms. Livengood, to celebrate all the kindness they had shared with each of them, and all together wanted to share some final thoughts with you.

Sam, age 14: "Look, and look some more. Buy a good magnifying glass. You'll be surprised to see that there's more to everything than you ever imagined."

Sue, age 14: "And take a good look at people. See them for who they are and what they really need."

Linda, age 19: "If you can move your hands and arms and legs and feet, you can dance. So, dance, especially when you are happy or excited, but also when you're sad and feeling down. Dancing can help you feel like yourself no matter what your circumstances or feelings. Even if you only move your hands and fingers, move! Dance!"

Donald, age 21: "Read, study, explore, think, learn. The more you can do, the more there is of you."

Celia, age 21: "Love. Be patient. Accept difficulties. Be patient. Love.

Max, age 21: "Don't think you know all about yourself when you're young. As you grow, you'll grow into more of yourself. Don't make really big decisions all alone. Listen to those who love you most, and look for people who have dignity and happiness. Learn from them."

Phoebe, age 19: "Winston Churchill, who led Great Britain through the Second World War against the Nazi regime, was asked after the war to give a speech at a school and all he said was, 'Never, never, never give up!' That is really, truly, good advice."

Ms. Livengood, age 48: "Live faith, hope, and love. Everything will come out right in the end."

Mr. Livengood, age 50: "Sometimes you, and your family, will be tested by sadness and great struggles. We all are. Know that you are not alone, not when you're lonely, not when it seems no one cares, not when there's no one who understands, not when there's nobody to talk to. God knows you, loves you, and will see you through anything and everything. To trust can be a great challenge. Trust."

And so, as we draw to a close this part of the story of the Livengoods and their friends, everyone felt that there must be one more song. They all looked to Mr. Livengood, who smiled and reached for his guitar.

"Coming up to this anniversary celebration, I reflected on the great joys and sad times we had together, all that we learned and discovered within ourselves, the ways we grew in body, mind, and spirit, the challenges we overcame, our failures as well as our successes. I've come to believe that the answers to the questions and mysteries of our lives were not 'blowin in the wind', as an old song has it, but rather are found with each other and also found within. So, using the melody of that old folk song, I wrote this for our final get together. Tomorrow we each go on to the next adventures in our paths of life. My lovely wife and I will hopefully have another 25 years together. We want each of you to be close to us on that journey.

Here's a copy of the words, please sing along and enjoy the familiar theme.

Linda, please feel free to dance to your heart's content.

How many ways can you keep your dignity?
On how many paths can you keep on living free?
And how can you become who you are meant to be?
Standing strong with others and searching deep within,
Always looking deep within.

Every human being comes with dignity.
It can't be taken away from you or from me
It can't be earned so when lost, where can it be?
Standing strong with others and searching deep within,
Always looking deep within.

There can there be dignity in the way we live,
if we make healthy choices and remember to forgive,
and if we keep serene with faith, hope, and love,
Standing strong with others and searching deep within,
Always looking deep within.

Part II, Who Are We – Standing Together

Chapter One – Together and Within

Josef and Miriam Livengood are having a glass of wine before dinner at their favorite restaurant. Tomorrow is Miriam's 50th birthday. She knows nothing about the preparations for a surprise party being completed in the restaurant's private room.

"Miriam, you look so downcast. I know you're sad because Donald and Celia are away on their honeymoon and Linda is in her final week with her dance company, but we'll talk with them tomorrow and Sam and Sue are still home."

Josef was trying hard to sound comforting and encouraging but he also didn't know that the entire family and friends were nearby, waiting to surprise them in just a few minutes. The party had been planned long ago with much adjustment to their schedules. They had all agreed: "We wouldn't miss it for anything!"

"I really miss them, Josef, and can't help remembering all the birthday parties over the years."

"Mr. and Ms. Livengood," said a waiter who had approached quietly. "I'm sorry to interrupt, but the manager would like to meet with you in the next room, please."

Miriam's first reaction was that there had been some horrible accident with her children and they wanted to bring the news to the Livengoods discreetly. The anxiety she had always managed with a strict exercise regimen and was usually able to keep beneath a calm demeaner surfaced in shaking and alarm. "Let's go quickly, Josef," she blurted out as she grabbed his arm.

They were led to the end of a short hallway and entered a dimly lit room.

"Surprise!" Family and friends with smiling faces and laughing eyes sang the birthday song with the final verse based on the one they had all sung when Sam and Sue were born.

> *Welcome birth-day to you,*
> *Welcome birth-day to you,*
> *Welcome birth-day dear mother,*
> *You've helped all our dreams come true!*

Miriam cried in relief and joy. Josef simply smiled in awe and pride.

After hugs and tears everyone quietly formed a semi-circle around the Livengoods and they took turns for a champagne toast.

Aunt Tu, a guest of honor, had coordinated all the communications among the family and friends and had made the arrangement for the party, including being sure that the Livengoods would be available at this place and time. Her introductory remarks were brief.

"Miriam and Josef, although I was away so much of the time when I was still working, I stayed in touch enough to know how you have kept love and togetherness strong in this family. Miriam, you have lived faith, hope, and love and shown us all what those look like in the face of sadness as well as serenity, loss as well as success, and with constancy in times of confusion and tension. Happy Birthday, dear!"

Sam, now 16: "Mom, you've been so patient with my quirky personality and always brought out the best in me. As the song says, you've always made my dreams come true."

Sue, also 16: "Mom, maybe you've thought that Sam was the only one who observed so keenly, but I've watched you my whole life. You are *the* model for composure and kindness. Thank you, and Happy Birthday!

Linda, 21: "Mom, you really wanted me to continue with my education but supported my love for dance. Thank you for your patience. My birthday present to you is that I'm "retiring" and returning to school to become a dance and movement therapist!"

Miriam closed her eyes and held Josef's arm tightly. He understood.

Donald, 23: "Even though your own education was discontinued so you could work to support your brothers and sisters, our education was always of the greatest importance to you. None of us would be where we are today without your support, trust, and encouragement. Happy Birthday, Mother!"

Celia, 23: "You've accepted me into your family. I am so grateful for that. I feel like a daughter, not a daughter-in-law. Happy Birthday, Mom!"

Josef brought a chair. He knew Miriam needed to sit down.

Max, age 23: "Like Celia, I've felt fully accepted, maybe more by you than by myself. Your acceptance has been a great influence on my life. Happy Birthday, and many happy returns!"

Phoebe, 21: "You're a never-give-up kind of person, Ms. Livengood. I toast your good health and long life and offer my gratitude because you've included me on family outings and vacations and given me a sense of peace and belonging that holds me up when I get discouraged. Happy, happy birthday!"

Mr. Livengood, age 52: "Miriam, I remember your words at our last grand gathering: 'Live faith, hope, and love. Everything will come out right in the end.' Words to live by and to trust. As Aunt Tu said, you have lived by that belief, and it has made each one of us a very rich person by being with you. Thank you for all you do for me and for us. May a blessed birthday be yours now with endless blessings in all the years to come!"

Ms. Livengood, age 50: "Josef, I especially remember two lines of your closing song you played and sang the last time we were all together like this:

And how can you become who you are meant to be?

Standing strong with others and searching deep within
Surely good advice to keep us from "Blowin' in the Wind"!

I am with the people who are most important to me, and looking within I can see that what I really need and want to do is dance. Put on the music!"

Chapter Two – A Full Heart for Max Again

I was privileged to be with the family and their close friends at this first "grand gathering" in two years. It was wonderful to see them all together. As they dance and get caught up with one another, I can briefly fill you in on the past two years.

Aunt Tu's retirement has certainly given her more time to be with the family, and she's a steady, trustworthy friend for them all, most of all for the youngest, Sue and Sam. Sue, especially, finds her a willing listener for the trials of the teenage years, as she calls them, and Sam appreciates being able to talk science to someone at great length, although as Aunt Tu would privately confess, she doesn't really understand everything that Sam says.

Sue has fully discovered that there are boys in the world besides her brothers and their friends. She still wants to be a nurse, a dream furthered by her volunteer work at a nearby rehabilitation facility. She especially enjoys working with the youngest patients.

With help from family, friends, and fellow scouts Sam has completed his Eagle scout project, a small indoor playground for "Sue's children" as he calls them. It includes a lab called *Exploratory* with large magnifying glasses and lots of specimens. Live animals include a gecko, turtles, fish, and "visitors" as he can borrow or catch them. So far, they've included two rabbits, a duck, three chicks, a puppy, a mother cat and kittens, and a garden snake. He's recruited and manages a team of retirees to clean the cages and tanks and keep the place in order.

Linda's dance group has kept her busy but as she says, "I'm glad I got that out of my system. Now it's time to put it to use to help people." She's been talking with a dance/movement therapist and will be starting school soon.

Her friend Phoebe has faced more discouragement that she wants to discuss. She returned from the Peace Corps to find that Max, whom she dearly loves, has "put the relationship on hold". She still wants to be a counsellor, but her enthusiasm, drive and determination have been dampened. Feelings of great loneliness from early in her life have returned.

Max is struggling in the management of his father's business since his father has become quite ill and isn't available very often to give guidance. He's working extremely long hours and can't seem "to get on top of it". He doesn't have time for a serious relationship and the self-doubt and lack of confidence from his childhood are constantly gnawing at him.

Donald and Celia are newly married and hoping for a pregnancy just as soon as it can be. Donald is a reporter, working long hours under pressure, and feels in a bind between researching and writing about a topic in depth and yet trying to meet all-too-short deadlines. Celia is working as a teacher's assistant while completing courses on-line for a master's degree in teaching. Even with the intensity of their lives, they're obviously in love and very happy. They were glad to come back from their honeymoon early for the surprise birthday party and are making plans to continue their "time together away " as soon as possible.

Tomorrow is a day of work and school, so there are hugs and kisses all around as everyone heads home. Linda catches Phoebe as they leave.

"Phoebe, we've been good friends for a long time. Something is wrong. Can we go for a walk and talk about it?"

"Sure", is all Phoebe managed to say. It's only a short walk to a park bench. The summer evening still has plenty of light and very few people are around. The friends sit still and quiet. Phoebe's hands are folded in her lap, her face down. Her long hair can't hide the tears. Linda waits.

"Linda, I think I'm pregnant. It's not with Max. The Peace Corps was a great experience, but a lonely one. When I came back, I couldn't adjust to the wealth and waste all around me. Everyone seemed so preoccupied about nothing that really mattered. All the suffering here is hidden or comes in outbursts, often violent. I couldn't fit in anywhere. One evening, like this one, in a park, like this one, a young man asked if he could sit down. I didn't have any friends, no one to talk to, so I said OK. Neither one of us said anything for the longest time, but I wasn't uncomfortable. Finally, he said, "The squirrels, those doves, that family over there, everyone seems just fine. I'm not. Are you? I looked at his sad and lonely face and said, 'No, I'm sad and lonely and don't feel hope for anything better'. He said, 'I'm better!' in such a cheerful way, that I laughed. It seemed I hadn't laughed for a long, long time. Then I cried. I put my head down and cried. He slid next to me and put his arm around my shoulder and put my head on his shoulder. I couldn't stop crying. He said, 'It's OK. I'm here'. He was kind. And gentle. He invited me to his place, and I went. Now I think I'm pregnant. He's nowhere to be found. You're the only person I've told. Max is too busy. My parents would be horrified. How can I have a child? Nobody wants me now, nobody would want me with a child. All I can think of is to have an abortion. Nobody would know. It's just a clump of cells."

Again, Phoebe and Linda sat very still and quiet. This was bigger than they were.

Finally, Linda said, "Phoebe, you're my friend and part of my family. We stand beside one another no matter what. I'll be with you in this. Please don't do anything right away. Let's think about this. We'll figure out the right thing to do. Honest. And Phoebe, it's more than a clump of cells, no matter how small. You know that. It's somebody. Growing. I'll do right by you. You do right by her, or him. Will you?"

Phoebe nodded. She didn't have any more tears.

"Phoebe, you've known Max a long time. You love him, I know. He's under a lot of pressure right now because his business may be failing, but he's a good man and he's trustworthy. One way out of loneliness is to let someone know about you. You've let me know. Let's let Max know."

"No!" Phoebe yelled. "He doesn't have time for me now, how do you think he'll have time for me when he knows I'm pregnant? No, no, no!"

"Phoebe, listen to me. Loving someone means trusting, it means coming out of yourself, it means being honest, being true, letting someone get close to you. Max is strong. I think he's strong enough to handle this. Let's not anticipate what he'll say or do or how he'll react. Let's give him a chance to be himself. Let's give you a chance, Phoebe."

"Linda, I'm so ashamed. I've let everyone down. Especially Max. I wanted to marry him, have children with him, and have a life together. I've ruined everything. I'm so ashamed."

"Phoebe, look at me."

Linda was calm and composed. "You're not *Ashamed*. You're Phoebe. You're my friend. You're pregnant."

Linda said it so matter-of-factly, so simply, so much without judgement, that Phoebe laughed. And then she cried with arms around Linda, cried with her head on Linda's shoulder, cried and sobbed until there were no more tears.

"Will you go with me to talk to Max?"

"Of course, but not at work. I'll set the time and place so we can talk for as long as need be, without interruption. And I won't tell anyone just yet. Max should hear this from you. Just promise that you won't get an abortion. And no more shame. We need a plan. Together. And that's where Max comes in. He's great at planning, even if his business is failing."

Phoebe laughed because Linda was so sure, so solid, so comforting. And she was right. Max really was very good at planning. And trustworthy. And strong. And she really did love him.

The next two days went quickly. Linda stayed closely in touch with Phoebe. The first part of her plan was easy. The problem was what to do with Sam. She thought the patio at her house was best for a private, and perhaps lengthy, conversation.

She simply asked Mom and Dad if they could go for a long walk or something on Saturday after breakfast. They understood that they were not needed for whatever Linda had in mind. Saturday was Sue's day to volunteer, but what to do with Sam?

"Sue?" Linda's voice went up a notch. "Would you need Sam with you Saturday morning?"

"Not really," Sue replied quickly, "because..." They had been close since Sue was a baby. She looked at Linda, then said, with a slow smile, "Well... now that you mention it, we have a few kids very interested in Sam's *Exploratory,* but I think they need some expert guidance so sure, I could use his help."

Linda gave Sue a hug and squeeze.

Saturday was a bit breezy, but nonetheless a good day for the patio. Phoebe and Max were there early and made small talk while Linda filled their cups with tea.

"Max," when the ready time was upon them, "we invited you to tea because Phoebe has something important to say to you."

Max looked very ill-at-ease, so Linda said, "Phoebe, are you OK? I'll be close by, in the kitchen."

Phoebe was clearly worried, but straining for confidence nodded and said, "Yes. Thanks, Linda."

She told Max the whole story, just the way she had explained it to Linda.

Max looks confused and uncertain and not at all self-confident. Then he noticed the apple tree, his favorite over the years. He said, "Phoebe, would you excuse me for a few minutes. I notice there are some small apples that should be culled. It will help the other fruit grow larger and make less stress for the tree. Maybe you could help Linda in the kitchen."

Phoebe understood his need to be alone. Max always needed a few minutes to sort out complicated or troubling things. She had always known that about him.

They could see Max from the kitchen window. He was culling the smallest apples, six could easily fit in the palm of each of his large hands, no doubt. It looked like he was talking. Or praying. Max had become a bible-reading, praying man ever since his dad's illness. He shook his head vigorously, then held his hands together, nodded very slowly, and turned back to the house. Phoebe and Linda hurried to meet him.

Nobody spoke. Finally, Max said, "Just like Joseph... in the bible. I'm like him. Upset. Confused. Uncertain what to do. Mary was pregnant, but he wasn't the father. But he loved her. He stood by her. He tried hard to be the best father he could be. Always.

Phoebe, will you marry me?

I know it's sudden, and maybe not the best time. I always intended to ask you to marry me, but when the business was on solid ground so we could have a secure start together. But this..." he paused and looked firmly at Phoebe, "is more important than the business. I've been thinking about nothing else day and night. I should have been thinking about you. I don't really have much to offer you right now. I'm sleeping in the back room, but there's room for you and the baby, and you could give it a woman's touch. I think it could be home until we can get on our feet."

Phoebe went to him, placed her hand in his, kissed him on the cheek, touched his face with her other hand, and said, "Maximus, you are the greatest man, greatest friend, greatest husband, greatest father. You are noble. I've always loved you so much, but now I love you more than I thought love could ever be. I accept and would be most proud to be your wife. If we're poor our entire lives, I won't ever care or complain. I'll love living with you in the back of the shop. I'll love you forever."

Max always remembered that hug, for it made him feel worth more than all the stars in the sky. His heart was full.

Chapter Three – Bright and Sunny

"Thank you for letting us know, Linda," Dad said. "We're honored that Phoebe and Max gave you permission to share such sensitive and personal information."

The entire family had gathered together at Linda's request.

"Max and Phoebe were too embarrassed to tell you about their situation, but they're on their way over right now because there is something Max wants to say, and to ask. There's the doorbell."

As Linda went to let them in, everyone sat in silence. Mother and Father held hands; so, did Donald and Celia. Sue looked confused and sad. Sam looked highly focused and resolute.

"Thank you all for meeting with us, especially on such short notice. No doubt you had to cancel plans for today. We're both humbled and grateful, yet we have a big favor to ask, well, actually two." Max was clearly self-conscious and very nervous.

Phoebe looked surprisingly bright and hopeful. "Max and I would like to get married as soon as it can be arranged, and we'd be deeply honored if you all would help us with the preparations and be involved in the ceremony!"

At that, the overall mood changed. Miriam, ever the grand matriarch, hurried to Phoebe, embraced her, reminded her that she was like a daughter, and started the planning as she led her out of the room. "Will it be a large or small wedding? I'm sure our pastor will allow the use of either the church or chapel. Where would you like the reception? You're welcome to our house. The patio is large enough and Josef would provide the barbecue. Let's go to the dining room table and start writing our plans."

Phoebe was happy, relieved, and eager to make the wedding more real through the conversation and the details. She was basking in the encouragement and support.

Linda was smiling so broadly, her cheeks hurt and she kept saying, "Phoebe, I am so happy for you!"

The men stayed together in the all-purpose room where Max was continuing the story. "My mother was surprised because I hadn't spent any time with Phoebe since Dad got so sick. I've been working 80 hours each week and have had no time for my martial arts, running, and only a little weightlifting from time to time. I worry about the business constantly and have lost quite a bit of weight.

Mom has been cooking and cleaning for me in addition to caring for Dad, so I know she'll welcome another woman in my life. 'Why the rush about getting married so quickly,' she asked and there was a slant to her head and in her words. She had it figured, so when I said that Phoebe was pregnant she didn't seem surprised, but I could see the question in her eyes. Phoebe and I had agreed that we didn't want to start life together with any secrets. To accept us means to accept the truth of our lives. I told Mom the whole story, exactly as Phoebe told it to me and to you. She had tears in her eyes and said she was extremely proud of me. That sure felt good. We decided to let Dad know about the wedding but not the pregnancy just yet. We'll wait for him to get stronger.

I mentioned that I had two favors to ask. The first was with help for the wedding. The second is actually much harder for me. He absent-mindedly ruffled his hair and looked dark and lonely.

As you know, our business is struggling. Failing would be a more accurate word. I'd sure welcome any ideas and suggestions you might have. I can't afford to hire a consultant, and I don't know who to turn to. Dad has decades of know-how, but his job right now is to get well. Would you help me? I don't even know what kind of help I need. I'm so tired I can't think straight. Fresh eyes might see something I can't."

It was obvious that it cost Max a lot to ask for help. He'd always been so independent, believing he could do anything, make any necessary changes on his own, simply work harder and harder until the business turned around. But it wouldn't. He couldn't.

Josef spoke first. "Max, we'll do all we can. The first thing is for us to see the day-to-day operations and look at your books. Miriam can help with that. She's had decades of experience with a complex household budget and runs a tight ship in money matters. After Aunt Tu switched from working in the field, she worked in the business end of publishing during her last years before retirement so she could put her other degrees to work. I know she'd be glad to help. I know he's young, but Sam has more interest in machinery and know-how than any of us. If he and you are agreeable, I suggest he observe out on the floor."

The only thing more noticeable than how tall Sam was sitting was his beaming smile. Max turned to him and said, "Sam, I'd sure like your input."

Sam was sitting on the edge of his chair. "Sure," he said as he jumped up. "There's a real leader among the adult volunteers at my *Exploratory* who'll be glad to run things while I'm busy at your shop. The scout troop is strong and doesn't need me just now. The ROTC program for the Navy doesn't start until the Fall and I'm well prepared for it. I have a lot of homework, but I can give you two hours after school every day. After books and computers all day, it'll be a pleasure to be around machines and get my hands dirty!"

Josef was the one sitting straight up now. You could see his pride.

"It's a deal, and thanks, Sam," said Max. The appreciation was strong and heartfelt, and Sam knew it.

Donald had been quiet the whole time, but he was thinking. "I've learned a bit about advertising during my internship and think I could help with that, but I'll need to get a close look at your products, get to know your employees, and become familiar with the competition. The problem is that my time is very limited. Could I just come and go whenever my schedule permits?"

"Absolutely! Welcome aboard Livengoods!" As tired as he was Max felt invigorated. "Having you all stand beside me makes me feel that we can do this. The forecast for the coming days is bright and sunny with the heavy clouds and strong winds simply vanishing."

Max shook hands all around and walked quickly to find Phoebe. He felt his old energetic self again after so long enclosed in the numbness of great fatigue.

Chapter Four – Relief and Happiness

For a young lady with so much sorrow, Phoebe came into a degree of self-assurance that surprised everyone, especially herself. She reflected often, with humility and gratitude, on the new-found responsibility of bearing a child, her confidence in having good plans with such strong and loyal friends, and most of all the unwavering love of Max.

The blessings kept coming for Phoebe. Her relationship with her mother took a sharp and greatly uplifting turn. They had been estranged for years. Her mother's depression made her unavailable for Phoebe during her adolescent years, the time she needed her mother the most because of her own fears, loneliness, and insecurity. Her father she barely knew. He had worked long hours six days a week for as long as she could remember. He was successful and a good provider of material security, but she never understood his unending drive for business and she knew that he never understood his only child.

With plans for a wedding and a grandchild on the way, Rivka's depression lifted as therapy and medication had never been able to do. Mother and daughter were both delighted with a warm and rapidly growing relationship.

One quiet day, Rivka confided her life story, and much about her husband, to her daughter.

Both had grown up as neighbors in a small village "in the old country". They were born just a year apart during the occupation by the Communists. Their families kept alive their peoples' history, culture and religion furtively and with fear. Isaac's mother made her own paints and created beautiful images of local scenes on small, smooth stones. At age seven Isaac began selling these artifacts, and as a small, very lean and always-hungry child he could get an even better "pity-price". He also developed a business sense that allowed him to drive a hard bargain. His little income supplemented what his father brought home from the village bakery and made a lasting impression on Isaac, his family and their relations.

"Yes, we were poor, but so was everyone else. Isaac and I planned to marry young. No one expected to live a long life then, but he worked in his father's bakery from the time he was 10, and as long as there was flour we wouldn't starve, he said.

His father sent him home for supper and to do his homework for our one-room schoolhouse, but he stayed late every night. One night, when Isaac was about 12, he returned to the bakery to get the pencils and notebook he left there. He was surprised to see the bakery dark, because he knew his father was still there. He had a key and let himself in very quietly, not sure what to expect. When he closed the door he heard a faint chug-chug coming from a back room he had never entered. Always a curious boy, and always trusting his father, he opened the inner door. Instantly the printing press stopped. His father quickly blew out the lantern, took Isaac by the hand without a word, closed and locked the doors, and they walked home. There wasn't a word between them.

At the end of the village, they turned through a gate. They had seen no one. Once inside their house, Isaac's father told him he must never mention what he had seen and what he now would learn.

The small printing press was similar to the one Isaac's grandfather had used to publish *The Thinker's Resistance* against the Nazi regime and now his father was carrying on the work against the Communist occupation. Grandfather had been arrested and was never heard from again, but Isaac's father had learned much about "the business" as it was called. He, too, had been a baker, but the place he owned was always referred to as "the bakery".

Isaac must always do well with his studies; his father told him. He must be smart and always discreet. He explained what that word meant.

Isaac resolved that day to be like his father, and when we were married I was accepted into his family and learned about "the business". They trusted me. My job was to take copies of the one-page, two-sided *Thinker's Resistance*, (the same name), to the university on the new rail-line. I left the stack in a locker.

After the Wall came down my father-in-law insisted that we leave the country. He was afraid of great disorder and reprisals from the authorities. He said, 'Go to America. Be free!'. Isaac agreed, but only because of me and because we wanted to start a family in safety and freedom.

Isaac's father's connections in the underground made it possible for us to get out of the eastern bloc, as it was called, and then on to New York city. We were still poor, but we had each other and Isaac's immense energy, drive, and determination. You were born in America, and we gave you an American name. Isaac's new responsibility as a father compelled him to work even harder. He worked in a bakery but also started one and then another small business. As his earnings increased, he started more small businesses, hired others to manage them, and slowly we grew out of poverty. I told him we had enough, could he stay home more? But no, he had an insatiable desire to provide the utmost in security for his family.

Finally, he had enough to purchase a small specialty publishing company that was going out of business. He was convinced he could turn it around and after a few years, he did it.

But there was a cost to his success. My parents had died, you inherited your father's sense of independence and determination and wanted your privacy, and I found myself alone and desperately lonely. I was a good homemaker but had no friends. I brought with me my old-world sense of secrecy and lack of trust for anyone outside the family. And you and Isaac were my only family."

Her mother looked at Phoebe with a trusting and vulnerable look of appeal for understanding.

Phoebe embraced her mother as she had not done for years, and they both cried in love, relief, and great happiness.

Chapter Five – "To Life!"

"Max, I like you," Isaac said. "I believe in you, that you'll make a good husband for my daughter. I know how hard you are working, but the Livengoods don't have experience in running a business -- God bless them for their goodwill and efforts. Thank you for letting me take a close look at your operations. I've made a study of your competition and frankly, they're much better positioned for success than you are."

Max looked crestfallen, but he sat up straight and continued to listen.

"I'd like to make your father an offer to buy his business. As you know, I own a specialty publishing company. It's doing quite well, but we need to grow to meet demand. Your site offers us some good potential. Your equipment is in good condition, and I think we could find a buyer. Your physical plant would accommodate the type of equipment and the layout we need. If your employees are interested, they could learn the new trade. I'd need a site manager. How'd you like to work for me? I'm getting older and promised Rivka that I'd figure out how to be with her more, maybe travel together, so if this works out you could become a partner in a year or so and gradually take over. I'd love to be a part-time consultant. If you're agreeable, together we'll talk with your father. Your wedding is in two weeks. I can make this happen in less time than that."

Max was stunned. He hardly knew the man. What a Godsend! "This is so much like my relationship with my father," he thought. "I can do this!" he whispered to himself.

"Yes. Yes! Thank you, Isaac!" They shook hands heartily. Max felt so much lighter he could have sung and danced. But he didn't. "Decorum!" he told himself.

It was only two miles to where Phoebe was waiting for him at one of their favorite restaurants, but Max didn't want to drive. He wanted to run. Fast. So, he did.

Max ran into the restaurant, startling some customers, and hurried to Phoebe. He was breathing hard as he explained his meeting with her father.

"Phoebe, your dad has the experience, the know-how, to make this happen. I can offer you a solid, dependable life. I'll have to work hard, but not 80 hours every week.

And I'm really impressed with your father. He's so... well-spoken. He's come so far."

Phoebe looked at Max and noticed not only how relieved and happy and how solid he was in himself, but also how deeply happy she was for him. What a blessing it was to her to be thinking and feeling for someone else.

Max's father and Isaac found a kinship in each other, both having struggled so diligently to raise themselves into success to support their families. "Let's call it a deal," they both agreed to a toast.

Max's father felt such a burden lift from him that he immediately felt better than he had for a long while. He continued to get stronger every day, for he had only two weeks until he walked his daughter down the aisle.

Isaac had always been a man of his word. To spend more time with Rivka, he sold his other businesses to a friend who had been after him for years to do just that. The money was invested to provide income for the two of them for the rest of their lives with enough to leave to the new family.

"Isaac," Rivka said one day. "I've noticed that you've been looking at me differently since you've retired. I do appreciate being with you more, but tell me what else is going on, please."

"I realize that I love you more now than I ever have, Rivka, and that for too long I haven't really paid attention to you carefully, to what you are saying, to how you see things. I haven't noticed that you have such good, practical ideas and insights. I'm coming to feel more open to you and to appreciate you more than ever. And you've helped me to learn to laugh at myself more often, a truly wonderful experience!"

Isaac's deepening love for Rivka, even after all the years of her great loneliness from his absence, had an ongoing healing for Rivka's heart and soul and health. She became ever more the person she was meant to be. She felt content, which she realized was a deep form of happiness.

The wedding was a "blessed blend", as Aunt Tu called it. Everyone had always accepted their variety of religious practices, but those came together so peacefully and naturally in the ceremony that everyone felt strengthened by the differences. Max's parish priest obtained for him a dispensation to marry in a neutral place, a small chapel by the lake that family and friends had so often visited together, and he attended as a family friend. A rabbi also attended, along with an evangelical minister, all seated prominently to afford them great deference and respect. Harmony among family members was not only preserved but strengthened by the sign and substance of such great mutual respect.

There were many endearing conversations that highlighted rich, complex realities.

This was Sam and Sue's first wedding. "We're looking, listening, and learning a lot, aren't we, Sue? The three L's."

"You forgot the most important 'L'," replied Sue, with a twinkle in her eye as she looked at her twin.

Sam was abashed. It wasn't like him to overlook or forget something. He noticed their mother and father laughing so hard they were holding each other up. "Laughing? Leaning on others?" he said, without certainty.

"No, silly," said Sue with a shy but very bright smile. "Loving!"

Together they moved closer to hear what Phoebe was saying. She had an authoritative air about her.

"Jesus, Mary, and Joseph were Jews, as were the apostles," maintained Phoebe, now an active member of Jews for Jesus, a Messianic Jew, while still celebrating Sabbath with her parents each week. Donald, a strong Evangelical Christian, agreed. "Yes, and your strong connection to your Jewish roots enriches our understanding of all that Jesus learned as he grew up in his family and community. Thank you for strengthening the power of my witness!"

Celia, Donald's wife, who attended services with him, was really a contemplative by nature. It was only the strength of her commitment and her courage that allowed her to be such an active pro-life advocate. But she needed some quiet time to explore the depths of all she had been reading and thinking. She hungered for spiritual guidance. She found a quiet moment to talk with Max and asked, "I've been reading about St. Ignatius and discernment. Can a non-Catholic make an Ignatian retreat?"

"Definitely," he quickly answered. It can be made at a retreat center, and there's a way to do it in your daily life. I've just completed one to get ready for this wedding. I'll send you some information and contacts."

And on it went, into the night, with singing, dancing and both excitement and relaxation. As Isaac said to Rivka on their way home, "This was a start to life, a culmination of life, a grand hope for life." He raised his arm high, "Lehayim -- to life!"

Chapter Six – A Story Ended

After the wedding everyone returned to their normal, very busy lives.

Josef and Miriam, having felt inadequate to help Max with his business although they gave it their best, were secretly grateful to be relieved of the commitment to the longer hours and pressure. Miriam had put aside the book she was writing and was eager to return to it. "The characters are waiting to be developed," she told Josef.

Aunt Tu has been going over Miriam's early chapters and preparing suggestions.

Josef had kept up his obligations with the university and with his students while earnestly trying to find time to help Max. He felt that he was letting him down by not doing more. "Miriam, we have a three-day weekend coming up. Let's get away. You really want to get to your writing and the mountains are calling me. I have two partly written songs that have been on my mind."

Donald got a promotion, which eased the financial pressures somewhat, and he was being called on for a piece of investigative writing that finally gave him a chance to combine research and writing, his two favorite activities. He supported Celia's desire to go on a three-day Ignatian retreat. "I'm so sorry you haven't become pregnant. It's been wonderful trying, but I know how disappointed you are. I'm saddened and confused, too. We've followed all the best medical advice and resisted pressure from well-meaning but misguided people."

"Donald, I don't mean this as a criticism because I love you just the way you are, but you sound like a professor sometimes, even when sensitivity is called for, especially when you explain things. I can see you teaching at a university someday, just like your father. I mean that as a compliment.

Anything and everything is easy for people to say, I know, but the heartache is still there. You know I share your impassioned defense of dignity of everyone, beginning at conception. I work with and study with people who make surrogacy and *in vitro* fertilization sound as if there's nothing wrong with those, even though they eliminate our intimate love for each other as the vital presence in the gift of life. (I feel like I'm explaining things the way you do. Marriage partners really do rub off on each other, don't they?!) It's so hard to listen to them. When I try to explain why those are wrong, they act as if I'm odd and I feel they stay away from me, as if I'm an antiquated nobody. I'm hoping that this retreat will help clear my mind and my resolve." Celia's voice was quavering, she had tears in her eyes, but her resolve sounded much stronger than she realized.

"Sam's volunteers" as his family calls them, have managed his *Exploratory* quite well and have set up an organization to further the work without them, or him, knowing how apt he is to find new projects. Indeed, Sam got intrigued working with the machines at Max's small factory and wanted to see the new equipment. Max hired him as an apprentice, so yes, Sam is moving into the world of work while still being a full-time student. He has never been short on energy.

Sue's boyfriend, John, is also interested in the medical field and is encouraging her interest in nursing, even though it would mean traveling aboard the USNS Mercy, a long-held dream. John is interested in being a physiatrist, a medical doctor trained in physical medicine, rehabilitation, and pain management. Sue is fascinated by more than just physiatry.

Linda's desire to become a dance/movement therapist has become even greater as she researches the connection to healing. She and Sue talk about this a lot, and it has further inspired Sue's focus in "her field", as she calls it. Linda knows she needs a master's degree and has begun exploring that objective. She is also a "full-time friend" to Phoebe, which is where our story continues.

Very early one stormy Monday morning with strong winds bending branches and clattering around houses, a phone rang repeatedly.

"Linda," she heard a tired and anxious voice say, "this is Phoebe. I'm sorry to bother you, but could you come over? It's been a very long weekend, Max had to leave early because they begin the transition of his business today, and I'm still worried and sad and upset because I had a miscarriage this weekend and…"

"Phoebe, Phoebe, wait a minute, please. Let me… I… I'll be over as soon as I can. Be brave, good friend."

As quickly as she could, Linda arrived to find tea and toast waiting for her and a more-comforted Phoebe with her face washed and long hair brushed.

"I knew you'd come. Max has been a dear, but I need another woman to talk to, and you're the best. Thank you so much for coming over at such short notice. I can tell I woke you up; I'm sorry. Please forgive me. I didn't know where else to turn." Phoebe saw the worried look on Linda's face and quickly continued, "Don't worry, I'm fine, mostly. I started bleeding more and more and Max was really scared. He wanted to get me to the hospital right away but I told him 'Just a few more minutes, please'. Before I knew it, I passed everything. Max didn't want to flush it down the toilet so he put what he could in a bowl and put it aside, then he took me to the hospital. They got to me quickly and explained everything and soon I wasn't cramping much anymore or bleeding much and really felt reassured. Physically I'm OK, but emotionally I'm mixed up. Max had so willingly taken on all this. He's feeling mixed up, too.

All along we called the little one Proto, or PB, (it even sounds like 'baby') for Proto-Baby, a beginner, earliest form of a baby, only about nine weeks along or thereabouts, we figured. We stayed in touch with PB's development and figured that he or she was developing all the major organs, hands and feet and eyes with muscles beginning to form, with a head almost 50% of his or her total length, to be as smart as Max, I said. You know, this whole time we never once talked about PB's origin. It's not forgotten, of course, but we have been so involved with PB's growth and preparing for the future that we both felt like parents.

Max insisted on having a grave site with flowers and a little plaque. I'm kind of feeling numb, except for some pain, so I'll gladly defer to him. We're just taking it one hour at a time. I have to see my doctor in a couple of weeks for an ultrasound to be sure all the tissue has passed. By then maybe I'll get a bearing on all this.

Thanks for listening, Linda. I feel better going over all this with you." Phoebe put her face in her hands and cried. She didn't know why.

Linda put her arms around her and let her cry, a soft cry, not shaking, but from deep inside her. Something, someone was lost. A story was ended without a beginning to take its place.

Chapter Seven – Getting Better, Getting Worse

Celia's retreat was wonderful. Most of all, she learned about discernment and resolved to "put it into practice all the time", as she told Donald when she came home. "I came to an understanding of myself, better than I ever had, as someone who not only wants a family more than anything else, but also as someone who can wait for God's will to become clear without so much anxiety, maybe without any anxiety. It's a kind of letting go, without letting go of what I most want, but letting go of a feeling of being compelled by my desire. My desire is deeper and I didn't know that. I am me and I am strong enough to live without anxiety. It doesn't do anything for me!" Celia laughed.

"I had a good look inside and I'm more empty than I thought and far more full than I thought. Thank you, Donald. Thank you, Saint Ignatius. Thank you, God." Donald felt a bit in over his head, but not so much that he didn't realize that it was time for a hug.

"A time for all things", he said to himself, feeling very proud of Celia and very much in love with her.

At about the same time, and not too far away, Max was holding Phoebe's hand and reassuring her that he loved her very much and everything would be alright.

Aunt Tu was reassuring Miriam that her first several chapters were really very good, and not to be discouraged about the lapse of time, that the pieces of her story would fall into place and that she would help her every step of the way.

"Donald," said Dad offering a question as an invitation to talk. "How was your hike and camp out?" Donald had taken a day during Celia's retreat to go for a backpacking hike on one of his favorite trails.

Douglas W. Price

"Wonderful! I really needed to get away. I hiked hard all day with a heavy pack to a small meadow off-trail. Pushing myself made it easier to let go of the pressure and frustration I've felt at work for too long. I'm happy being a journalist, and this new assignment will give me a chance to prove I can do in-depth work.

Dad, I have two questions for you: Celia says I sound too 'professorial', especially when I should be more sensitive toward her. And secondly, she's so upset about not being pregnant yet, we both are, so how should I treat her? What do I say? I know how much this means to her."

His father was still and quiet as he thought. He prayed for the right words.

"Donald, let your love for Celia and your love for life and your belief in dignity for everyone guide you. It's easy to say, 'learn to relax under pressure' and not something that I've mastered even after all these years of trying, but the stress you're experiencing may be carrying over to your personal life. When you, and I, feel something is important, or when we get under pressure, we tend to get a bit formal and academic, stuffy really. Be in touch with your love for Celia, for your profession, for all that is so important to you, and don't concentrate so much on the content of what to say. Speaking from love is more enriching than any textbook talk could ever be."

Josef could see that Donald was listening, thinking, trying to accommodate this guidance into the way he is. No small task.

"Son, I know you're tired. You look worn out. Your first report is not due for another week. You have high standards and expectations for yourself. Is it possible that you're the one putting so much pressure on yourself? Even your hike was a form of stress, good stress, but still another form of hard work. Why not take the rest of the day to relax and do something you enjoy, just for fun, a real human need, you know."

And that's just what Donald did. He read a Western story from the Sackett series by Louis L'Amour. It had nothing to do with any of his obligations or his work. Or maybe it did. Later, he told himself, he'd see if his younger brother Sam wanted to go for a bike ride on some dirt trails up to the lake for a swim after work. He could help him with his homework later. Donald enjoyed that.

Sam needed a break, too. He had been keeping up his schoolwork "admirably", his dad said, but he was taking his apprenticeship so seriously that, despite his youth and indefatigable personality, he was becoming worn around the edges.

"Sam," Isaac put it straight, "you've been at this long and hard and doing a fine job. My new man is an outstanding salesman, but he wants to work with the production end of the business, too, so I want you to take a few days off, full pay. I know you ride your bike to school and to work, but I also know you like to ride the dirt to the lake. Go for a ride this afternoon, just for fun and some balance in your far-too-serious young life." He said this with his hand on Sam's shoulder and with such an encouraging smile that Sam saw the wisdom and affection and quickly agreed.

When Sam got home, he rushed to the kitchen for a snack, but was stopped when he saw his mother and Linda in what had apparently been a serious conversation. He mumbled his apologies for the interruption, grabbed some fruit and homemade bread and hurried back to his bike.

"I think Sam knew we were talking about something important. For all his laser-like focus on tasks and projects, he's a pretty astute observer of human beings," Ms. Livengood said with a soft smile and appreciation, "and I am so glad that Phoebe is doing so much better, but my mind at the moment is on Isaac and how run-down and weak he's been looking."

Chapter Eight – Standing Together

His doctor was blunt. "Isaac, your recent tests showed very troubling results. You need rest, extended rest. You've continued to push yourself too hard, against my recommendations, I might add.

Please. At least a month. No work. Absolute rest. Take a vacation. Have some fun, Isaac. You're a good man, but far too serious and hard-working, even in semi-retirement.

After a month, very gradually build up your activity again. And Isaac, let go of worry and so much responsibility. I've known you for many years. You carry responsibility in your mind all the time, and unfortunately in your heart. Isaac, your mind may be strong, but I must tell you that your heart can not, will not, keep up the way you've always lived. Let your son-in-law run the business, by himself.

After just a few days, Isaac said, "I can go back to work. They need me. There's so much to do".

Phoebe assured him that this was the time for Max to take over completely, that Isaac had prepared him well even in such a short time and that as they had done for Max's former business, the family would step in to help. Rivka was insistent and as she held Isaac's hand she said, "My dear husband, I know you have been through many trials in your life and have always managed through hard work. This time it must be through the work of others who love you. Who are we, Isaac? We are the ones who will be with you and stand with you in whatever comes. Let us help you. Let us love you." Isaac looked at his wife of so many years and trusted her, loved her, and was ready to follow her lead. He actually didn't feel very well at all.

"Yes, dear Rivka. You are right. I'm fearful of rest, actually. I've never rested long. I'm not sure what to do with myself. I'm afraid I'll be seen as lazy; I'm afraid I'll start feeling lazy. This troubles how I think about myself. Pray for me, Rivka. Please pray for me."

Much to his unending surprise, creative talent Isaac didn't know was within him surfaced. He studied his mother's small paintings on smooth stones and decided to give that a try. He was painstaking, as with everything else, and had an intuitive feel for color and design. He was pleased at the quality of the results.

And once again, relationships blossomed. Max's father visited Isaac almost daily, as a brother would, and Sam became the son he never had. Isaac enjoyed long conversations with someone besides Rivka for the first time in his life.

He began to see himself differently, and so did others. A long-time customer told Isaac in such a relaxed and friendly manner, "You look much younger, my friend." He had never called him "my friend" before.

Isaac found himself smiling and laughing more and talking to strangers, something he rarely did before. He said "Good morning, beautiful day" to those he passed on his daily sunrise walks, which often led to wonderful conversations.

Through great diligence, Max was able to keep the business prosperous without Isaac's help, and loyal customers found in him not only competence but a strong, welcoming and dependable business relationship.

Isaac worked hard at regaining strength and vitality, as he had done with everything else in his life, but he relaxed much, much more. It took quite a while to achieve this balance, but persistence was always one of his greatest attributes.

He tried activities he never imagined him self doing. Max introduced him to Tai Chi which Max practiced as a martial art, but Isaac was quite satisfied with practicing the forms for balance, centering of his intense personality, and calm control within movement.

Linda introduced Isaac to a psychologist in whom she had great trust. They formed a wonderful friendship, and on a long walk in the mountains Isaac asked, "Is it possible for an old man to become a new man, not actually a completely different person, of course, but... how would you say it, *revitalized*?"

They walked for a few paces before the answer came. "Yes. It is."

One day, over a cup of tea, Rivka said, "Isaac, I've always said that there's a silver lining to every cloud. What is it this time?"

Isaac didn't have to think long. "A stronger family and I am stronger within it. I have even more love in my life with relationships that are fresh. I'm a better man.

Rivka understood Isaac so well. They had been through so much together.

"You love and you accept our love. I see your gratitude for this. There are many who love you, Isaac. We have a large family."

Isaac looked solemn.

"Rivka, my Dearest, ever since I was a little boy I have needed money, for myself and my family to live, to be secure. But somehow that need came to be more of a desire for money, for the certainty it could provide, to keep away all worry and fear, to dominate life's problems, to be so strong that nothing could conquer me or my loved ones. Rivka, money somehow became almost an end in itself, just to have more.

My poor health could not have been prevented by any amount of money, and though the medical help I received did cost money, the deeper healing that I'm receiving comes from love and friendship and from blessings of growth and insight. I don't want to say I'm glad I got so run-down and so close to a heart attack, oh no, but I feel that I am a better man, husband and father, and now have a more clear sight for what is most important, what I really want: to spend my remaining days with you and Phoebe, and now Max, and the entire Livengood family, giving my best to each one, to give freely and receive freely. Yes."

Chapter Nine – Well on the Way Home

"No! I don't want to go for a bike ride with you, and I'm tired of everyone being so nice, so kind, so willing to help everyone in the world, so *on top of it* all the time. I'm not on top of anything. I don't want to graduate from high school. I don't want to go to college. I don't want to be a nurse. I don't want to have anything to do with the medical profession, or even helping other people. So there!"

Sue stormed off to her room. Sam heard her door slam. He didn't know what he had said, other than to offer to go for a bike ride with his sister. He knew how much she loved to ride, or used to anyway, and thought it would help. She was not at all like herself, he thought, and hadn't been for a while. He didn't know what to do. Should he try to talk with her? Slip a note under her door as they had always done with each other and with their parents when tensions flared and talking wasn't possible? Sam always knew what to do. But he didn't. He knew his father was very busy grading final essays, but this was important. He knocked quietly. His mother came to the door.

"Mom, Sue's finally lost it. She yelled at me. She never does that. I just offered a bike ride to get her mind off her troubles, whatever they are. She looks frustrated and miserable. She said she doesn't even want to graduate or be a nurse. I don't know what to do."

Ms. Livengood stepped aside and motioned to Sam to come in quietly. His father was at his desk, running his fingers through his hair, looking harried, Sam thought. "Did I just make a pun?" he wondered to himself with a wry smile in spite of the troublesome situation.

He saw the five piles of essays his mother had made for each class, her traditional way of pre-sorting for grading. She always put aside her own work at end-of-term to help his father with the load he brought on himself by assigning a lot of student writing rather than the multiple choice exams much easier to grade. His topics were cumulative of the semester's work, very demanding, and legendary. Dad turned with a pained expression, but he turned all the way to signal his willingness to postpone his work for Sam's concern.

"I heard, Sam," he said. "We've all noticed how on edge Sue's been. Snippy. Abrupt. Sarcastic even, which she's never been. It's time for a family meeting."

They gave Sue time to calm down. Mother fixed an especially good meal, which Sue barely touched. As they cleared the table Dad said, "Sue, the dishes can wait. Have a seat."

Sue looked sullen and angry, but she sat down hard, arms folded across her chest. Nobody spoke. Mother cleared her throat when she knew that Josef was at about eight on a slow count of 10, and she said, "Sue, dear, for quite a while you haven't been your usual cheerful self. Something's not right with you and we want to know what it is."

Sue looked at her mother and father, scowled at her brother but saw his innocent face, and burst into tears.

"John says he doesn't have time for a girlfriend. He's got to concentrate on preparing this summer for a 'grueling load', he calls it, getting ready to begin the path to medical school. He loves me, he says, but he doesn't want me to love a failure. He says he knows he isn't the smartest or highest-ranking student in our class and that he'll be with even smarter students in college next year and he doesn't want to be left behind. He's even given up soccer and swimming. He's so dutiful and focused it's disgusting. He's kind and thoughtful like Dad, purpose-filled like Donald, and Sam – he's got super concentration like you. Why did I have to pick such a problem for a boyfriend."

Sue laughed, then cried, then pounded the table hard, once. "I am so angry and mixed up. I don't know who I am anymore, or what I really want. I feel dull inside one minute, and then so full of sadness and frustration that I don't know what to do about anything, anything at all.

Sam, I'm sorry I yelled at you. You deserve much better than that. I know that you, all of you, and Donald and Linda love me and want me to be happy, but I'll tell you this. There's not an unhappier person around."

Dad started his silent count to 10 again. Everyone waited.

"Sue, I don't want to talk about John just yet. I want to talk about you. In times like this it's very important to remember who you really are, and how much we are with you, standing with you in any confusion or any feelings. And yes, to remember that God in Christ is with you always. So, take heart, dear daughter. And listen carefully to me now, please.

I'm going to tell you what you are not remembering as your feelings and confusions loom so large in your life.

"Sue, when you and Sam were born, we sang this song." He looked at Miriam and she took the cue.

Welcome birth-day to Sam,
Welcome birth-day to Sue,
Welcome birth-day dear children,
You are our dream come true!
A little boy are you,
A little girl are you,
We're so happy you're with us,
You are our dream come true.

Her mother quickly added, "We've never stopped feeling that way."

Dad smiled, nodded slowly but assuredly, and continued.

"You've always been a loving person, and have shown that in so many ways. Sam, for all his brilliance, didn't talk for a long time and he didn't need to. You spoke for him. You were so in touch with his needs and moods that he never wanted for anything, and though he was even more energetic than you, stronger and more assertive in many ways, you were always protective of him."

Sue looked at her brother. He saw her embarrassment and smiled at her. She smiled but fought back tears.

"And you knew where and how to look for a model for your life. You admired your mother's kindness and composure, traits you've developed in yourself, yet always knew how to be exuberant, singing and dancing for any simple occasion."

Sue no longer kept her arms folded but held her hands in a relaxed posture and sat with her back straight. She looked thoughtful as she tried to remember years and precious times gone by.

Do you remember how much Aunt Tu helped you research the USNS Mercy hospital ship, and how much she encouraged your interest in going to very poor countries? You were shocked and upset that so many people never get medical attention and wanted to do something about it. You resolved to help them as a nurse on that ship. You and Aunt Tu even took a tour on the Mercy when she was in port not too far away."

Sue realized she hadn't thought about this for what seemed like a very long time. She remembered how she felt, how important it was to her, how much her aunt shared her interest and what an adventure they had together.

"Now I want to talk about John for a moment." Sue looked like she was going to cry again.

"No doubt he sees in you the qualities we do. No doubt he admires what makes you, you. I can tell you a lot about the past and present, but I won't even venture a guess about the unknown, mysterious, wonderful future, but I do know for sure that the one person you are always going to take with you into your future is yourself. Don't lose yourself, Sue. Keep true to who you are.

Look inside yourself and look at the solid relationships in your life. Your family has always been there for you and always will be. It sounds as if John is flooded with worries and is anxious about his future, his ability to succeed and be proud of himself. My guess is that he wants you to be proud of him. Remember, Sue, he is young, too.

It's time for some serious and very careful thinking, isn't it?" Dad and Sue looked at each other for a long minute. She went to her mother and father, hugged them, then went to Sam.

She stood before him for an awkward moment, but spontaneously they reached out for each other at the same instant.

Sue was well on her way home to where her heart lies.

Part III: We Rise – Stamina and Stability

Chapter One – So Much to Do, So Little Time

"Josef, you're more like a brother than a friend." Isaac paused. He sounded hoarse, only partly due to the vigorous hike to the 8,000-foot overlook on the trail they used to hike twice a month, but hadn't for quite a while. It was not a popular trail because there were more direct routes to the summit, and so they had the solitude they both enjoyed.

"I need to talk about Rivka.

You've all noticed her forgetfulness and the vagueness that comes over her, like a mental fog. She's always been a realist. I call her My Sacred Realist. She's always been a prayerful person, but since her diagnosis a couple of years ago there's a been a definite increase in symptoms. She was doing well for a while and so happy that we had so much more time together. She was invigorated, actually! But time came a year ago to let everyone know how things really were, and you all were so understanding. I'll forever remember how you rallied around her and me. Phoebe and Max are still coming to terms with it, but they've done a lot of research, and their regular visits are friendly and uplifting. Everyone has offered all they can and this has made life easier and better for us. But I think you know all this. I'm working up to something.

Increasingly Rivka gets disoriented and frustrated. Sometimes when I ask a simple question, she gets mixed up and confused and gives a wrong answer to something she should know. She repeats words and stories she's told but a short time earlier. Even with the best medical help, she's getting worse but I see it more than anyone because I'm with her all the time. Rivka has always known how to get along with others in an unobtrusive, non-offensive way. She had to learn that as a little girl, so it's an instinct. Unless someone gets in a deeper than 'how-are-you-doing' kind of conversation with her, her Alzheimer's isn't readily noticeable.

Phoebe knows and understands because she sees her more than anyone. She is a patient, attentive, and kind caregiver. It's wonderful for me to see their relationship, so much love and trust. Max is so much more a son than a son-in-law, and his parents have been involved and supportive, too. Sue has been amazing. She's learned a song or two and some simple prayers in our native language, and when Rivka is vague and lost songs and prayers from her childhood bring her back to us. Linda gets Rivka moving and clapping and dancing and singing and for a short while she's so excited and happy, but she gets tired easily. And sometimes she seems anxious and afraid, though none of us knows why.

You've heard parts of this I know, but since Miriam broke her leg skiing you've been pulling a lot of double duty and you and I haven't been on a hike for a long while. I really appreciate being able to say all this to you.

I love Rivka and she knows it. Often, we just sit and hold hands. She is comfortable and peaceful and relaxed and trusting. Josef, I'm scared of what this disease can lead to, most of all to the possible failure of her recognition of me and Phoebe, and I don't know what to do about it. I feel that you're the only who can share this burden with me."

Tears slid down Isaac's cheeks. Everyone in the world only saw the strong, confident, successful, never-give-up Isaac, the one who could conquer anything. Isaac the fearless. Isaac the indomitable.

Josef felt both alarmed and honored to be in this moment with his friend.

They sat quietly for several long minutes, neither knowing what to say.

"Josef, it helps so much for you just to listen. I don't feel all alone with this. I know you care, and I know you understand."

Isaac took out a much-worn half-sheet of paper. "This is a poem that Celia wrote for me. May I read it to you?" Josef nodded and Isaac began in an unsteady voice.

<u>Orientation in Alzheimer's</u>

*God is telling me something in this vague world
into which I retreat. Pardon me
my confusion, my embarrassment, my failure
to understand you, my irritability.
I cannot discern the path I should take
in my thoughts. Next steps are unclear
and yes, I vacillate between fear
and aggressiveness. I understand nothing,
yet I trust, when my breathing is steady,
that seeing God's way is immanent.
In this moment, perhaps, before it is over,
I will see. I will see, and understand
and be so very happy.*

Celia is very intuitive and in touch with Rivka's moods and feelings. She comes by whenever she has time. Rivka looks forward to her visit. Celia gives her soft but dramatic readings of children's rhymes and songs. They pray together using the prayers Rivka has known from childhood. Rivka loves their time together. The vagueness falls away and there is alertness and the old Rivka.

This poem means so much to me because it's Rivka from the inside out, what she feels and how she sees but what she can't express. I sense its deep accuracy. It's very painful, yet it brings me close, across all the frustration and anger, anger at myself."

Joseph wanted to talk about this, but he knew enough to let Isaac speak without interruption.

"All in all, I have so much to be thankful for, but it is hard. When I'm alone I'm often sad and filled with regret for the years of time together lost because of my insatiable ambition to become wealthy. I know, I know – the drive and determination and endless work gave us the security and prosperity we so much needed and the freedom from hunger, freedom from fear, freedom to be ourselves. But there was a trade-off. And I miss Rivka so much already. I've not said that to anyone else, so thank you for letting me say all this to you my friend, my brother."

Josef was so greatly saddened by his close friend's misery that he couldn't speak.

"Josef, there's something I'd like you to do for me. I have lived so much inside Rivka's life this past couple of years that I've been out of touch with your family, like unto my own family in so many ways, except for brief visits by those who are nearby. The others come to see us when they visit you, and we've learned that just a few friendly minutes count for so much. I'm afraid the door for even those may be closing because it may be that everyone is becoming a stranger.

So, my brother, please bring me up to date with everyone's life. I miss them, miss knowing how they're doing, miss having people in my life."

Josef was relieved to be able to do something for his friend. He began. "I'll start with the youngest first because I know they hold a very special place in your heart.

Sue is 19 and in her nursing program. She's kept a fixed purpose. You'd be proud of her. She told John that she could help him in his studies if he'd let her, but otherwise she has her life to live. Such resolution woke him up to her strength of character and her help and support has helped him relax. They're both doing well and set for the long haul. Although Sue hasn't admitted it yet, I think she's ready to follow him wherever he goes.

He comes from a good background. John's father is a fine man. Very intelligent. He reminds me of Sam, wide interests yet with a laser focus. He dearly loves his son and twin daughter, Joan. He's a dedicated doctor and researcher but has deep misgivings about the time away from his family that his profession requires. We've invited them to a picnic at the lake next weekend and look forward to getting to know them all better, especially the twins' mother whom we don't know well yet. She spent a lot of time with the children growing up, especially with their education. Incidentally, John and I are meeting this afternoon for a quick bike ride to the lake. He wants to see the picnic site. His father is at a conference all day regrettably, but we have his blessings.

Sam is also 19 now, and highly valued in the specialty publishing business you gave to Phoebe and Max. You know how well they're doing, but you may not know how Sam is valued by your employees. They've kind of adopted him as their kid brother, but with a lot of respect for all his innovations, some so simple, some patented, but all yielding improved efficiency and productivity. Since so many of his ideas have to do with workplace changes and personal productivity, Sam's turned his interest away from machines and production to industrial psychology. He says, 'Dad, I think I've done what I can without a lot more specialized education and training, but human behavior is fascinating, and I really like the people. It's endlessly intriguing to help them get better at their jobs, and it's fun." He talks like his father the professor, but I feel pretty narrow in comparison. There's no end to his interests.

Linda, 24, is finishing the master's degree she needs to become a dance/movement therapist. She loves the field and is very talented. It turns out that her instincts to join a dance group after high school were sound. The experience developed stage presence to help her overcome shyness, and that opens a lot of possibilities for her. She has a mentor, and an internship promised upon graduation.

Donald and Celia, both 26, are doing well and have started the process for adoption. They've accepted it as the only way they'll have children and are grateful for the opportunity. They'd like to adopt a baby, but the wait list is long, so they're considering older children as well. You probably see Celia more than anyone because she is so caring and generous with her time for Rivka. Donald has had two promotions in fairly short order and is now an editor. Their financial situation has stabilized, and he tells Celia he wants her to be happy with her volunteering and he's fine with being a one-income couple.

We are all so proud of Max and Phoebe. He continues to work as hard as it's possible for anyone to work, but he's listened to your advice and gives your daughter the time and attention she needs. Phoebe genuinely enjoys working in the business and she and Sam make quite a contribution to the high morale of their workforce. In fact, it is such a high-energy workplace that the employees have turned the tables on Sam and give him so many ideas to research and develop that he's having the time of his life. He's always been solitary in his pursuits. Now he's a team member, and he loves it. In my visits to "the shop" as everyone still calls it, it always appears busy and highly organized with no time, effort, or material wasted. Everyone gets along well and the humor along with the drive and determination would make you proud.

Lastly, the old timers. Miriam is still in her early fifties, but I'm about your age, 55. She's well, has finally finished her second book, and is searching for a publisher. She really enjoyed writing a novel, but it's a crowded field and her traditional values don't play real well in today's market. She and Celia team up for volunteering at the pregnancy resource center and Miriam feels that their relationship helps Celia. As you may remember, both her parents are deceased and she has no siblings.

And as for myself, I'm older and slower but still enjoy racing. I've never been competitive, nor an athlete, but training for an event 'ups my game' – it makes me more fit. I love to swim, bike, and run, so triathlon is a natural for me, but even in my age group I'm no star. But I keep doing it.

As to work, I love teaching and imagine I always will. As you know, I've taught a variety of levels and subjects, but I confess that I still think about other opportunities. So much to do, so little time!

Chapter Two – A Good-Advice Team

With Josef out for an early hike with Isaac, followed by a bike ride with John, Miriam and Phoebe were starting their day over a leisurely cup of tea in their favorite café. They had been talking over an hour and were just getting warmed up. It was "half-throttle" Saturday at the shop, so Phoebe could be spared.

"Miriam, Linda mentioned to me once that you and Josef wanted a large family when you were first married." She was surprised at the feelings her question evoked, and paused in respectful silence and some regret that she had asked what was evidently a highly personal question.

Miriam recovered quickly and naturally, smiled and said, "Yes. We both wanted six children. But we're very happy with the four we have. They're wonderful."

Phoebe waited because she sensed there was more. Their relationship had been strong, and she wanted to know. She, too, wanted a large family. As an only child, she had always looked longingly at classmates who had brothers and sisters. They seemed so happy and well-settled.

"Phoebe, to tell you the truth, motherhood comes instinctively to me. I find myself drawn to that type of close relationship with you, with Celia, with the young employees at the shop and pregnancy resource centers, and certainly the troubled women who come there for help. I don't think about it, it just comes out in conversation. I find myself wanting to encourage and help people, to help them get on or stay on a path to realize their hopes, their dreams, their potential. I like to listen to people and somehow that leads them to talk to me honestly about whatever is on their mind. I used to resent the time that shallow or superficial conversation takes, but then I read that almost 90% of communication is non-verbal: eye contact, facial expression, gestures, posture, pacing and pausing and tone of voice. That really changed my outlook, and I realized that people ease into conversation, not even consciously necessarily, so they can assess how comfortable they are talking to you, whether they feel honesty and care, whether they can trust you, and how much. Finding out interests, experiences, ideas and values help a person choose topics and decide a level of acceptance. And people watch your reactions. They'll often float out a tidbit that's revealing or controversial and judge by your reaction whether they can go deeper. It's really quite a study, yet it all takes place in seconds or minutes before a go or no-go signal develops or closes a relationship. It sounds formal and abstract to say all this, but it's so important because it's a way that people find common ground, friendship, encouragement, support, and validation not only for their thoughts and feelings but for their very selves."

The women got up for a stretch, to get more hot water, to let it all rest for a few moments, for Phoebe to sort and sift and fit all Miriam's understandings into their relationship, for Miriam to feel the weight of everything she said that summarized so much of her life.

"Josef loves teaching and the research and writing and relationships that are so much a vital part of teaching. I love relationships and the research and writing and conversations that help me understand relationships. As you can imagine, we have some very lively conversations. He helps me understand how to help people. I help him learn more how to understand people. A match made in heaven!

"Oh, Miriam, you're a such a gift!" Phoebe had known her for years and had felt her compassion and dedication to helping others. Now she had a better understanding.

The two shifted back to lighter subjects, updates on how family and friends were doing, and plans for the summer. And then Sue found them.

"Mother! … Hi, Phoebe…I'm glad I found you, both. I'm sorry to interrupt, but may I join you? I'm feeling a bit beside myself and it'd be great to talk about it."

Miriam and Phoebe exchanged a quick check of the other and both said, "Sure".

Without missing a beat, Sue continued, "Phoebe, I think you know about my boyfriend John. What you may not know is that he's a fraternal twin, just like Sam and I are. How's that for improbable!

Mother, you know that his twin's name is Joan, but what you don't know is that both of them were named for saints who were very strong, courageous people. I had met her a few times but just came from a long and wonderful conversation with her. John had to go to a study group and left us alone. She is *not* shy. Now bear with me. I am coming to a point here, a few points here, really. There's a huge point about John I'll get to for sure, but there's something about Sam in this that I want you to know and I want your advice."

Miriam and Phoebe smiled at each other.

"Go on, go on…"

"Well, Joan wants to be a sociologist. She wants to get her doctorate and teach and research and write, like Dad. She's been focused on courage her whole life, she says. Their father is a medical doctor at a research center – I never did get exactly what he does there – but his interest in courage has been a guiding light for Joan ever since she was a little girl, and for John, too.

But I'll get to him later. I want to get to where Sam comes into the story."

Miriam and Phoebe were trying to look serious, but kept grinning in pure happiness at Sue's impetuous enthusiasm.

"So Joan mentioned, among about a hundred other things, that she's a cyclist and loves to run and swim and do oriental martial arts. I said, 'Oh, you should meet my twin brother, Sam, and I told her all about him. Now, here it is. Joan really wants to meet Sam. She wasn't saying it to be polite. She's like him.

She's enthusiastic about everything, I mean everything, just like he is, except she's unbelievably sociable and he's a hermit, well, not really. But he is solitary. Well, he used to be, but his Eagle Scout project and the *Exploratory* and working at 'the shop' have brought him out of himself a lot more.

So what do you think about that. Joan really wants to meet my brother?"

Without waiting for an answer, without more than a quick breath, Sue continued.

"Now about John. As Mom knows, we've become very close. Very close. In fact, … I haven't told anyone…but… I love John AND he loves me! Yes, Mother dear, your youngest daughter is in love." She notice her mother's expression. "Well, maybe you kind of thought it all along…

Anyhow, here it comes, John doesn't really want to be a doctor at all."

Miriam and Phoebe looked surprised and unsure about what to say.

"He really wants to be an elementary school teacher. He loves kids. His experiences at summer camp, Sunday school, and tutoring have inspired him far more than the medical profession. He knows how important that is to his father, who's made no secret his whole life about how proud he'd be to have his son follow his footsteps, so being the dutiful type John headed down that path.

Now you're probably wondering what my part is in all this… well, I'll tell you. Two days ago, I said to John 'What about your namesake, John the Baptist? Wasn't he known for his courage? Doesn't your father value courage at the top of the virtues? Wouldn't he admire courage in his son? Isn't truth a cornerstone in courage?' I let him have it. I was really wound up because for so long John has been suffering in shoes that are too tight for his feet, with a hat that's the wrong style for him, for going in the wrong direction. Don't you see what I mean?"

This time, out of breath, Sue waited.

Miriam said, "Yes, dear, I do see what you mean. You're trying to help John be who he is, not who he thinks he's supposed to be."

"O, that's what I told him, and I could tell he liked to hear it. So, John, in his usual careful way, said he'd think about it and knowing him, I figured he'd do just that. He'd think long and hard and wrestle with it. I can't imagine Joan or Sam doing that for more than a few minutes. But sometimes I think I'll be an old maid before John reaches a decision and acts on *that*. So, I planned to ask you what I should do about that slow hard head. 'But maybe he'll surprise me', I thought. You know, when John makes up his mind about something, he's very firm in his decisions and action. And guess what? He called me this morning to say that he talked to his father and mother last night and they've accepted his change of life plans! How amazing is that. Miracles do happen!

But now the actual advice I need is how to set up a meeting with Joan and Sam. You know how shy he is around girls. He told me once that he's never met an interesting girl. He says he's met pretty ones, virtuous and not-so-virtuous ones, careful and careless ones, smart ones and girls afraid to be smart, but never an interesting one. I think he's afraid. Afraid-of-nothing Sam, afraid of meeting an interesting girl. And Joan is definitely, certainly, unequivocally interesting. So how do I get Sam to meet her. They'd be a match; I can tell you that. They'd be so busy with studies and research and projects and sports they'd never have time to kiss." Sue blushed and laughed at her joke.

Phoebe, a good listener herself, had waited for her turn to talk. Here it was.

"Sue, I think you just created a good-advice team."

Sue brightened up. She liked the expression.

Chapter Three – What a Day!

"Josef, I love sunrise hikes, even short ones, but although Donald and Celia were kind enough to sit with Rivka so I could join you, I must be getting back. She'll be sleeping, but I don't want to be gone too long. Donald has work to do and Celia is working on a piece she's writing, and they've brought their computers, but still – I am interfering with their plans for their day off.

I really enjoyed spending time with you. My mind is more at ease than it's been for a long time. The fresh air, probably."

They both knew it was much more than that.

"Isaac, it's not too far back to the parking lot and you know the way. I'll go with you to where the trail splits. Would you mind going the rest of the way by yourself? I have some thinking to do."

Of course Isaac was agreeable and glad to do this small favor for his friend. He knew that Josef knew he was in good enough shape to handle the return hike by himself.

They hiked down the trail in silence, and at the appointed place extended a firm handclasp.

"Peace be with you my good friend."

"Shalom, my brother."

Josef watched Isaac go. He had more feelings than he could name. A lot had been accumulating with him over the past weeks. He needed some time alone.

The day was still young and the old, almost never-used trail he wanted was just what he needed. Quiet. Peace. Solitude.

Josef was used to going it alone in the wilderness. He had done so for many years. Hiking hard was a time-tested way for him to shed worries and pre-occupations so he could think clearly. Was Miriam really alright? She was still limping but always said, "I'm fine". How best might he advise Donald who seemed troubled by his new position? Sam shifted from one intensity to the next effortlessly it seemed, but was he going to be able to chart a steady course in life? And Sue? She is so independent and strong-willed. She's going through the ups and downs of her first serious love and sometimes seems out-of-balance. Is there fatherly advice he should give his young daughter, or let her alone? Linda! So talented, so capable. As the middle child has she been left on her own too much? She is alone so much. Is she lonely?

He looked at the three small photos of each of them he carried in his wallet, as he did from time to time. He especially liked seeing and remembering the children when they were very young. He loved each of them so very much.

"As for myself," he said to the squirrel who was observing him from a branch on a spruce tree, "I've been teaching the same courses for quite a while. Am I getting stale? Is the 'zip' gone from my focus? Can I awaken the love of learning? Inspire a career path? Teach content that truly makes a difference in the lives of my students?

I'm finding myself impatient, irritated, annoyed by little things that never bothered me before. What does all that mean?"

He felt a little too grumbly to sit still, so he hiked on until he could hike no more. Sitting against a large log off-trail, he looked through the songs he had written and recorded on his phone. Listening to them brought him back to a good sense of himself when he became discouraged or lost within sad thoughts.

This one he had written the last time he had hiked alone, after an illness. Hearing it brought back vivid memories.

Climb

Alone on a hill as a man can be
who's hiked off trail to see what he can see
and dwell awhile with juniper and rock,
gaze at cliff face and play a native flute,
thank God for his breath and strength for the climb
with regained health and enjoying more time
to have and to hold all that's good to see

for mind and soul and all a man can be.
Two blue jays in a pinyon tree.
Up or down there's slippery scree.
The hill is steep, the day is clear.
Animal tracks show who's been here.
Mine's the urge to seek and to find,
to stretch and roam, to sing and climb.

Josef did something he could never do with others. On clear, level ground with outstretched arms he spun around, six times clockwise, six-time counter-clockwise. He used to be able to do ten. Great for his balance.

There was enough time to meet John for their bike ride after lunch, so he stretched out beneath an aspen tree. He loved to look at the sky through the leaves…

He startled awake. He must have dozed off. A quick check of his watch let him know that with a bit of trail running he could keep to schedule. There were a few level stretches and even a couple of uphill runs (much easier on his aging knees), and he loved running trails. Time to be off…

His short bursts of running fast through the trees and meadows gave him more pleasure and inspiration than he could hold. As he pushed himself, the complexities of his life fell away and there was only room for exhilaration and gratitude and a prayer of thanksgiving when he stopped to catch his breath, and petition: "So many people look up to me, depend on me, need my support. Please help me, Lord." The sense of help was there, and he felt capable.

Arriving home rested and recharged, he quickly made the transition from hike and run to bike. "A kind of triathlon," he smiled to himself.

He made it to their meeting place to find John resting comfortably against a tree with book in hand.

"Hey, John!", he called as he rode up.

"Hey, Mr. Livengood!" replied John with a smile as he stood up quickly.

"What's that you're reading?"

"The Fellowship of the Ring by Tolkien. I'm beginning his trilogy. Sue's insisted that I read for enjoyment instead of studying all the time and she recommended this. There are such deep levels in Tolkien and his writing. I read his biography and letters before starting the trilogy so I could know the man behind the writer and the writing, and it really does help."

"So, you study even when you're reading for fun?!" smiled Josef with genuine appreciation and respect.

John felt the respect and knew that in a way this was Josef giving a compliment, for he knew from Sue that Josef was a long-time admirer of Tolkien.

"Yes, I study everything. You don't know my sister Joan yet, but as you'll see we're opposites in so many ways. She's brilliant and picks up insights and meanings quick as a swallow over a pond. I'm a beaver who chews long and builds slow and steady."

"Good imagery, young man! What do you think of Tolkien so far?"

"I'm reading him slowly because staying in touch with the levels of his thought is like getting to know Sue. There's always more than meets the eye," he said with a big grin.

Josef nodded with appreciation. "Well, what say we ride?!"

The two men, young and older, got on their bikes and headed to the lake. It was only another 12 miles but with some hills, so when they arrived they were ready for a rest.

Each brought healthy snacks and plenty of water. A picnic table at a lake overlook gave them a good setting for relaxed conversation.

For almost an hour Josef tried to keep in mind everything Miriam had taught him about the stages of conversation and non-verbal communication as people find common ground and trust.

"Mr. Livengood, thank you for meeting with me like this. I want you to know that Sue and I love each other. Our views on every topic we can think of are similar, or if not, we can disagree with respect.

We're committed to honoring each other by waiting until marriage, which we've discussed, and we do have a wait because I've followed Sue's advice and last night I told Dad and Mother that what I really want to be is a schoolteacher, not a doctor. Dad took it hard at first because he's always told me what a great profession it is and how fulfilled I'd be in helping others, which he knows is important to me. I confessed that studies for pre-med have been really difficult because I'm just not that interested. I don't think I'm cut out to be a doctor.

I respect Dad and the profession greatly, but I told him that what I really love is teaching kids, seeing them get excited and proud of themselves about learning, seeing the spark of their curiosity get connected to the natural discipline required for rigorous learning. I told him that I want to start working with young children so I can learn about learning in its beginning stages, and then move up through the stages of development and teach different grade levels and subjects. I think that would be good background if I ever wanted to be a principal to help shape overall school focus and culture. I shared with him some of my experiences of working with children, many of them funny, many of them simple, all of them touching something deep and vibrant in me, and as I talked at length I could see the tension and resistance in Dad begin to relax.

Mother really helped. She held Dad's hand the entire time. Sue's always telling me to observe people carefully. I tell her I always think about what people say, and she counters with, ' I said observe, not think'. She says there's much to be learned by just looking carefully at people. So, I've been trying. Last night, even though I was nervous, I noticed that when Dad, who's normally very controlled but calm, would start to fidget, even just a little, Mother would rub the back of his hand, and he'd take a deep breath and relax. When he'd glance at her, she'd nod and smile and he'd smile, just a little. I know they love me and I could see it within the stress of that conversation, and I could see how much they love and trust each other, too.

At the end we just simply sat quietly before he finally said, 'Son, it sounds like your heart and mind are set toward this, and I will do everything I can to help you.' If you knew my father, you could understand that this was hard for him, a sacrifice, truly generous.

Mother added, 'Son, we're very proud of you. We know you put a lot of careful thought into this, so we'll be with you all the way. We know this took courage'.

At that it looked like a small jolt, a kind of sudden reminder, hit Dad. He sat up straighter and said, and I'll never forget the sincerity in his voice, 'Son, always do what you think right and best for yourself and others. Rely on your courage and trust in yourself and God to carry you through.' With that, the deal was sealed.

Mr. Livengood, I'm 19 and ready to start my second year of college and am changing fields, so that's off to a slow start. But I'm a hard worker and can make up time because, as my dad says, 'my heart and mind are set on it'. Sue and I will wait until we graduate to get married, when I'm settled with an adequate income. As my father says, I'll never be rich, but we'll have each other and we'll be happy. With that, Sue and I don't need to be rich."

This was a lot for Josef to think about. "What a day this has been," he thought.

What he said was, "John, I'm honored for you to have shared all this with me. Like your father and mother said, Ms. Livengood and I will do whatever we can to help you and Sue and be with you all the way."

John's slight tilt of his head, the softening of his eyes, the relaxed but firm smile told him that his future son-in-law was a man of feelings anchored in right relationships and genuine sincerity that had the strength to go the distance.

Chapter Four – "Truth to Me"

"Josef, I really like your surname, Livengood. What's its history?" They had been talking with increasing openness for about an hour. John's father, Justin, clearly sired the highly inquisitive nature of his children. It seemed there was nothing outside his range of interests.

"It's Swiss German, from Lebengut, which means 'living good'. As you know, anti-Semitism has a long history in Europe. My ancestors converted to Catholicism generations ago, another unpopular minority at that time and in that place. Grandfather Nicholas, named after the saint who was known for successfully promoting peace in the 15th century and subsequently fostered a lot of conversions, saw the rising tide of antisemitism prior to World War II and, living in a neutral country, was able to obtain visas to emigrate to the United States. Unfortunately, he found antisemitism here, too, but was able to open a grocery store, work hard, and build a future in relative peace and security.

We're looking forward to getting to know both you and Josephine at the picnic this weekend. I understand she's from Uganda. Is she named after Saint Josephine Bakhita?"

"Ah, what a wonderful question! Yes, although very little known here, my wife's namesake lived less than 100 years ago and is widely loved and respected in Africa as someone exemplifying tremendous courage and kindness. My wife takes that heritage very seriously and I have to tell you that she's my inspiration for those virtues. She and I have tried to pass those along to our children. It's been such a pleasure to see Joan become so interested in courage. As I believe you may know, she wants to be a sociologist and study examples and influence of courage in families, communities, and nations. It is with both humor and admiration that we listen to her ongoing ideas for a dissertation topic – and she's only a freshman. John is quieter about his enthusiasms, but nonetheless serious about courage and kindness as guiding lights. We're very proud of them both.

I met Josephine at a conference. She was assisting an elderly doctor who needed some help with his English. I was smitten immediately by her poise and clear, but subtle strength. It took a bit to arrange an introduction and she politely but consistently rebuffed my initiatives, but my genuine interest in her companion doctor's specialty won her over, at least enough for dinner together. With great tact she handled my perseverance in such a way that I had to prove a depth for my attraction. I learned a lot about how a woman can draw out the best in a man and thereby help him grow. It took quite a while, but I'm forever grateful to her. True love is certainly so much more than a 'flash in a pan', isn't it?"

"Yes, indeed. I first saw Miriam in the library at our university, or I should say the first dozen times that's where I saw her. She was so focused on her studies I thought she didn't even notice me. What kind of introduction can you manage with someone who is so exclusively interested in her studies?

But then I got a break. I met her at the bike rack. I could tell by her bike that she was more than a just a casual cyclist. So here was my opening at last. I asked her if she'd like to ride the pine trails with me, a not-too-challenging course that would allow conversation. She demurred, saying that she was taking an overload of courses and working a part-time job, but thanked me with a friendly smile. So I said, 'Well even seriously busy people need to eat. How about dinner tonight?". She laughed such a relaxing and wonderful laugh that I was, as you say, smitten.

It was a slow but steady courtship and yes, I agree that a woman who takes her time can help a man develop greater strengths and maturity. 'Test for the best' I advise my daughters. So hopefully Sue and John are growing as they're coming to know each other."

"I think they are," Justin said immediately, with conviction.

"I know we're drawing to a close, Justin, but I want to say how much I appreciate getting to know you, and to thank you for your trust in encouraging John to ride with me to the picnic site last weekend and for helping me with some clean-up and repairs this afternoon while you're at the clinic. He should be home well in time for dinner."

"Certainly, my new friend. Your daughter is understandably very precious to you and Miriam and knowing her very steady boyfriend and his family is important." Justin looked at his watch. "Ah, well, I'll have to dash. See you at the picnic."

Because he needed to bring some tools to clear tree limbs downed by the recent storm, Josef had driven rather than riding to the café, the meeting place to pick up John, the same one where his wife, daughter, and Phoebe had recently had such good conversation.

He didn't have far to go, and was gratified to see John sling some tools in the back and hop in the truck with a familiar air.

"So how did it go with my dad?" No small talk today.

"I really enjoyed getting to know him better, and Miriam and I are very much looking forward to spending time with Sue, you, him, and your mother at the picnic.

I can see how you and your sister have developed such broad interests, yet with a strong focus in so many."

John said, "And now it seems matchmaking is afoot. Sue is super-keen on getting Joan and Sam together. It might be similar to a nuclear reaction, but with fission and fusion alternating as they talk, talk, talk – sometimes disagreeing vehemently, sometimes agreeing with more excitement than their poor little skull-vessels can contain."

"Ah, such imagery, my young friend. Good thing we have a cooling pond nearby!" Shared laughter broke any remaining tension.

They drove in silence, each with his own thoughts,

When they arrived at the lake, John said, "Whew – we have our work cut out for us!"

And work they did, long and hard, with no time for even casual conversation.

It was late in the afternoon when they completed the clean-up and repairs. Tired, they sat on a bench and drank as much water as they could hold.

"Mr. Livengood, since Sue and I are so serious about each other, there's been something on my mind for a very long time that I've never talked about to anyone. I don't know if it's any kind of impediment to my relationship with your daughter, but may I talk with you about it?"

Josef nodded his assent, eyes looking into eyes to find trust.

"When I was about 10 years old, I had a good friend. We had a teacher who was strict and humorless. The classroom was always quiet so we could pay attention and learn, but fun wasn't part of our academic life, for sure. My friend was so funny, and when we were together on the playground, in the cafeteria, before or after school, I gave him my complete attention and most of that was spent in laughing. Anyhow, one day when we lined up to come in from the playground, another boy who was watching our antics called out for everyone to hear, "John *loves* ---! with a smirking, sing-song voice. It caught on and I heard it more than once. Well, it was true, I had great affection for my friend, like I suppose I would've had for a brother if I had one. Anyhow, time went on and it was forgotten until I got to adolescence, when I remembered the incident anytime I liked a boy for a friend. It scared me. A lot. I didn't know how to approach or talk to girls. They seemed to live in a different world. I played handball and football with boys and that was my world outside of homelife and studies. I simply didn't know how to be open and honest and relate to a girl.

So, I've always wondered, am I a repressed homosexual? Sue is the first woman whom I've loved, been close to, cared deeply about, but I'd like to clear this up and my parents, as loving as they are, are so strict in their moral code that I can't even imagine talking about this with them. You seem more relaxed about sexuality and my biggest clue to that is how easily

Sue can talk about it, but I'm not going to bring this up with her. So, I'm stuck. What do you think?"

Josef didn't want to take too long to reply so he said, "First, John, thank you for trusting me enough to ask. Second, please bear with me because my family tells me that I can get too 'professorial' sometimes, especially about important topics.

I think, and feel, that we should approach this by talking about love. Do you know the story about Jonathan and David, in the bible?" Josef could tell that John was unsure so he continued, "It's a long, complex and very interesting story, but I think I can find a line that pertains."

Josef went to his truck and took out a bible, brought it to the picnic table and opened to Samual 1, 18:1. *Jonathan's life became bound up with David's life; he loved him as his very self.* This had absolutely nothing to do with sexual love, believe me. Please read the entire story. I think you'll like it and see a very action-oriented love and loyalty and willingness to sacrifice between two men.

"Secondly", and here Josef flipped quickly into the New Testament, "in John's gospel, 13th chapter we see this: *One of his disciples, the one whom Jesus loved, was reclining at Jesus' side.* As you know, Jesus talked about love a lot, but never homosexual love. Please read this reference, too. There are

many, many other references to love, which Jesus exemplified in countless ways.

Now there are two perspectives to be considered. Sexuality, in its healthy and all-too-often in its misunderstood and unhealthy expressions, is a driving fascination in our culture, and the development of sexuality in adolescence and young adulthood is an urgency to be understood, to be respected, to be honored and blessed in proper time and proper relationship. Everyone has struggled with its powerful force. It's one of the great dimensions of human personality and human existence.

I think your feeling of love for your friend when you were 10 is a tribute to the strength of your feelings. It means that you are a person capable of loyalty and love. It was a deeper and more sincere form of friendship than the all-to-often superficial friendships between and among boys and men. So don't be afraid of this, be grateful. It is a gift and is yours to value and to develop.

Like all feelings and all forces there are good expressions and bad expressions. What are guidelines for us? The best ever written begin 'Love is patient, love is kind...'. I know you're familiar with that.

Another place to look for guidance is in Natural Law. Here it is held that sexual union in marriage between man and woman is the proper expression of sexual love. That is your focus and your commitment, you and Sue. So you're on the right track.

Lastly, feelings can be guideposts, but true love, reason, and faith are our enduring guides. You have to decide which guideposts will lead you to the right place, which ones are in keeping with your values and beliefs and the values and beliefs that have been strongholds for humanity throughout its history on earth, and which ones have led so many astray into the wide paths of becoming lost and wronged. So no, I don't think you're a repressed homosexual. I think you're a young man who loves and who wants to understand love."

Josef looked at John, who was smiling.

"Thank you, professor, and I mean that with the utmost respect. You've spoken truth to me and behind and within your words I can tell it's because you care and want the best for me.

You've set my mind at ease. I understand and feel the rightness in what you've said."

Without another word, as if on signal, both men, the young and the older, picked up their tools, took one last look around, and loaded the truck.

On the way John said, "Just one thing about the picnic you may not know. Sam and Joan are invited as a couple." He looked just a bit smug, in a respectful way of course, at knowing something the professor evidently didn't know. They drove home for dinner, the only sound an occasional chuckle from Josef.

Chapter Five – A Foundation

Storm clouds and wind passed through the night, and with the dawn came promise of a clear day for the picnic with family and friends. Everyone was excited to be all together again, and each had a personal purpose to heighten interest.

Miriam was really looking forward to meeting Josephine. She had heard so much about her from Sue and John, and now even from Josef after his meeting with John's father, Justin.

Josef was feeling the honor and the pressure of being the patriarch. Family leadership had come naturally to him and he realized the importance of being sure that everyone felt included and comfortable. He was most looking forward to Sam's meeting Joan. He was happy for his son to find someone like himself. He was so strikingly unique and therefore alone, though always so busy he didn't seem to mind. Josef had high hopes for Sam finding companionship.

Donald and Celia, Max and Phoebe, Sue and John had announcements of great personal importance, though each couple didn't know that about the other.

Linda was looking forward to seeing Isaac and Rivka, who had not been at any kind of gathering since her diagnosis. The plan was for Rivka to be visited gently by family members in the Quiet Cove, as they called the small arbor behind the picnic site, and for Isaac to take her home if she became unsettled or afraid. Ever the concerned therapist, Linda was to be Isaac's ally in keeping Rivka feeling safe and comfortable. Isaac had seen many of the family individually as they came to visit, but he had been homebound taking care of Rivka and had not seen "his family" together for a long while. For herself, Linda was hoping there might be some time to talk to her mother and to Josephine together. There was a young man she was seeing as part of her dance and movement therapy sessions about whom she was both intrigued and troubled. He's a marathon runner from Africa studying in the U.S. What little she knew of Josephine, and what she definitely knew about her mother, suggested that they would have insights and guidance, maybe more together than if she talked with each separately.

Sue and John were at their first full family gathering as a couple. This new identity was thrilling for Sue, but a large family gathering was somewhat disconcerting for John. Sue had been reassuring his shyness for weeks and he had to admit that his curiosity was overshadowing his self-consciousness.

Sam and Joan had been told so much about each other by well-meaning match makers that they were at the height of curiosity and nervousness. Although different in so many ways, the 'striking uniqueness' of each, as Josef would call it, seemed to align with the other's very well.

Justin and Josephine, John's parents, felt genuinely accepted and welcomed by Josef and Miriam, yet trust is always somewhat fragile as it develops to a sturdy foundation for lasting relationships. Their innate openness to new experiences and affection for Sue gave them enough confidence to look forward to meeting the rest of the family.

First to arrive, Josef had many self-appointed duties. After thoroughly checking the picnic site, he set up equipment and mentally prepared to be the official greeter.

As family and friends began to arrive he welcomed each, offered refreshments, and gave a brief overview of locations for kayaking, volleyball, horseshoes, and provided a trail map. He knew he could count on his family to help newcomers feel at-ease. He noticed immediately that everyone introduced themselves and quickly started friendly conversations. Since he knew Josephine the least, as soon as she arrived with Justin, he made a point of welcoming them and bringing them to Miriam who was talking earnestly with Linda.

"Linda, John's parents, Justin and Josephine, have been looking forward to this picnic. You'll be glad to know that among her many talents Josephine performs dances from her native country." That's all he needed to say to Linda to initiate an eager conversation.

"Justin, shall we leave the ladies for a few minutes? I'd like to show you the kayaks and the 'lay of the lake'". That was an easy exit, and as they approached the dock they could see Sue and John well out into the water.

"What a great way to work up an appetite," Justin said. "Sam and Joan have already appointed themselves grill-masters and I noticed the homemade pickles and watermelon. What say we do some paddling?"

Josef needed no prompting. He needed to work off some energy, for he'd have to confess to some apprehension about this event during the weeks of preparation. They each took a single kayak, struck off from shore, and waved to Sue and John who had been first on the lake in their double kayak, but made a point to head in a different direction.

Donald and Celia, Max and Phoebe stood somewhat apart in the shade of some large pine trees and appeared to be in serious but happy private conversation and the others could see at a glance it was best for the time being to leave them alone.

Sam and Joan were indeed busy and well-organized at the grill. They seem to have settled into efficient teamwork, but their occasional laughter was a sure sign they were enjoying having something to do together.

After a brief but vigorous turn in the kayak, Sue and John were volleying the ball across the net in a friendly and relaxed manner, but with considerable concentration. "No spikes" seemed to be a rule, which was a good thing because John's arm span was just about the same as Sue's height. Sue was trying hard to measure up, and John's encouraging comments kept her relaxed but at her peak effort. "Good job, Sue!" could be heard frequently.

Isaac and Rivka were the last to arrive, and Miriam had been watching for them. As they moved slowly toward the goings-on, Miriam excused herself and met them half-way. She knew what Linda had in mind to discuss with Josephine and could catch up later.

"Isaac, Rivka, how good it is to see you!" Miriam's greeting was so warm and welcoming that Rivka smiled shyly and Isaac felt attracted to this very active scene. "I have a table and comfortable chairs in the Quiet Cove waiting for us. Please come with me." She adroitly led them away from the activities and helped them get settled in the calmer setting which would feel more secure to Rivka. Miriam stayed with them, spoke directly to Rivka, listened patiently, used all the body language cues, and never interrupted or corrected her. Isaac noticed all this and the effect it had on Rivka.

At a comfortable pause he said, "Rivka, I'd like to bring us something to drink. OK?"

Rivka said slowly, "Yes, please, Isaac dear" in such a clear voice that Isaac began to relax at the picnic, which in some ways he had dreaded. The last two days had been difficult.

As he moved away quietly, Miriam continued the conversation and was enjoying Rivka's peacefulness and earnest attention.

As Isaac searched for drinks and small snacks, he saw the tall woman in colorful clothing, Josephine in her Ugandan colors. He'd like to meet her and wondered how Rivka would react. The traditional folk dancing dress of their native country was also colorful, though not so brilliant.

Josephine and Linda had moved well past the "preliminaries" as Miriam called them, and were well into the conversation that Linda so much wanted.

"His name is Benjamin. He's a marathon runner from Kenya. Well, was. He fell hard during a training run and has been told that he'll never run competitively again. He's crushed. His physical injuries are healing well, but he talks to no one, even though I've been told his English is very good. He rarely smiles. He doesn't participate in my dance/movement classes. He only looks at me briefly, and then from soft, mournful eyes. Not what you'd expect from a tough competitor. He's isolated in his misery and that's certainly not healthy for anyone. He writes and draws a lot, but he doesn't show anyone. I looked over at his drawings once or twice. They're very good. He's close to my age. He's not married."

Josephine noted the inclusion of the last information, but passed over it and said, "Linda, I may be able to help. Our countries are only about 500 miles apart and we both speak Swahili. Most important for your work, Africans love to dance. I teach traditional Ugandan dances. I'd like to meet your friend, Benjamin."

Linda was stunned with excitement. For a moment she couldn't respond, but quickly recovered her common sense and gave Josephine the date, time, and location of her next session with Benjamin at the rehabilitation clinic.

Josephine closed with, "I'll come in traditional clothing for dancing! See you then!"

Linda's sense of relief and gratitude surprised her. "After all, he's just another client" she told herself. Something inside her didn't believe the way she said that.

Linda and Josephine joined the others around the grill and tables for lunch. Cheerful friendliness was in the air. Everyone felt good about seeing one another again, and about having a beautiful place free of obligations or interruptions making it easy to create or deepen relationships.

After lunch, Josef called for attention.

"Please get comfortable for some important announcements."

First, to everyone's surprise, Sue and John came forward. Their parents had been told beforehand and gave their full support to what was coming.

John spoke first. "Sue and I look up to Donald and Celie, Max and Phoebe. Their love for each other in their marriages, their perseverance in setbacks, and their strength in facing discouragement are models for us. Their relationships with each other and family are deep for solid footing in life."

It was Sue's turn. "Marriage is not only a union between man and woman, but also a bond to show family, friends, and community that love for each other is strong, protected and secure. It is in this spirit that John and I wish to announce to you, dear family and friends, that we are engaged to be married after we graduate and are ready to start a family. We're in in for the long haul, and that begins officially today!

Cheers and toasts all around! John and Sue walked off to hugs and well wishes.

Donald and Celie came forward and allowed a few minutes for everyone to settle down from that good news. All sensed a big moment. The only sounds were countless birds who seemed happy, too, and an easy wind in the pines.

Celie spoke first. She raised both hands to the sky, tilted her head back, and sang in a clear, strong but wavering voice, "I'm pregnant!"

Knowing how important this had been for so long for them, everyone stood up, clapped and cheered. Donald and Celie walked among them all for hugs, kisses, and tears.

At the right moment, Josef called out, "There's more! Please be seated."

Max and Phoebe came forward. Max began, "Phoebe and I are close in so many ways. One of those ways is that we share the experience of being so fully accepted into your family we almost feel like blood relations. Please know that you have made a life difference for me."

Phoebe spoke up. Tears were upon her cheeks and in her voice. "Your love and support have helped us to be the people we were meant to be, and it is with gratitude that I share the news with you that I am pregnant with our child -- Mom and Dad, your grandchild." She ran to Isaac and Rivka, who had been told beforehand so as to prepare Rivka. She understood fully and couldn't let go of Phoebe.

Sam was enthralled. An intellectual by inclination, he felt his emotional side blossoming quickly, "like time-lapse photography" he thought to himself. He turned to Joan who was sitting close to him. "Joan, would you take a walk with me?"

Unlike her customary assertiveness, Joan had been feeling shy around Sam, though she had been quick to carry her share of conversation. "Yes, I'd like that," she said looking at him with calm confidence. They had been inseparable all morning, and Joan found that she liked that.

As they walked the Pine Trail away from the sounds of congratulations and happiness, Sam reached for Joan's hand. Strangers only the day before, she willingly took his hand, the first time in their lives either had done this.

They walked in silence to a place along the lakefront that Sam had visited many times when he wanted to think through the scope of a project, or simply to be alone. He was filled with the presence of feeling and the hope for a future of not being so alone anymore.

"Joan, shortly before I woke up very early this morning, I had a dream. I saw a boy and a girl on a beach by the ocean, alone. The sun was low in the western sky. The boy, and maybe the girl too, had their arms outstretched and were singing, or chanting. I couldn't make out the words, but the feel of the words was with me as soon as I awoke and I wrote this."

He took out one of the note cards he always carried to write thoughts, ideas, insights as they occurred. "It's called *I You We*, said as one word. Please know that I've written lots of reports and documents. I've never written anything like this. I didn't know as I wrote what I was doing, actually. I didn't understand the words. Their meaning has been growing on me, in me, and I'm beginning to think that the words have something to do with us. Somehow I was hoping that even before we met." Sam took a deep breath, let it out slowly, and sang, or rather chanted.

> *Iyouwe*
> *Iyouwe, Iyouwe cried the sun to the sea*
> *let us go to receive I-with-you, you-with-me*
> *with time and space for us to play*
> *to think and feel and know and say*
> *I with you and you with me, Iyouwe, Iyouwe!*
> *There is little and much, more and then less*
> *we will free our hearts, I will give you my best*

*you must give all you have and whatever you will
while all of time grows and space is then filled
you and I find us, we find you and me -- Iyouwe, Iyouwe!
The sun sets burning away into the sea
time keeps spinning for you and for me
we are a blessing right now, a gift always for us
to have and to hold, a matter of trust
I with you and you with me, Iyouwe, Iyouwe!*

Sam felt unsure of what to do or say, but he was at peace. He felt he had given a gift to Joan, but he didn't know exactly what it was.

Joan sat very still. She felt her heart beating. She heard a dove in a nearby tree. A hummingbird came to her small yellow pack and hung in the air, searching. As he flew away, Joan and Sam smiled at each other. Sam really didn't know about girls. His sisters were sisters. Joan felt that everything she knew, or thought she knew about boys, didn't apply. Neither said anything.

Joan hummed the chant softly. It was in her mind, her memory, and her feelings.

Sam spoke slowly. "Joan, would you be my girlfriend?"

Somehow Joan wasn't surprised at the question, and without hesitating said, "I'd be honored, Sam." She leaned over and kissed him lightly on the cheek. And somehow, Sam wasn't surprised.

They got up from the bench and walked hand-in-hand back to the picnic. As they approached, Sam's mother was walking toward them.

"Sam and Joan," Miriam said as if she had just said, "Of course". The pronouncement was in the same tone of voice and cadence as she would use to tell someone, "Sue and John are engaged".

Josef was at a short distance, talking to Joan's parents. Miriam held up a hand like a wave, like a sign, and the three of them came over. They, too, could see what Josef later described as an appearance of completion, of something ended and something begun, something of life importance, of life's importance for his young son and his friends' daughter. Words couldn't add anything, so they all turned to walk quietly to join the others and as they did so they heard the sound of several all-terrain vehicles rushing up the road, which came only to this picnic area and no farther.

As the five vehicles came into view, family and friends reached for their walking sticks, all of them strong, smooth oak made and given to them by Donald, each with the initials of the new owner engraved at the holding end.

They stood together to meet the new arrivals, not sure what to expect but not liking the boisterous intrusion.

One by one the ATVs came to a stop and shut off their engines.

"We came to have a picnic," said the apparent group leader, appearing belligerent and intoxicated.

No one answered this challenge but simply stood quietly but resolute.

Josef stepped forward and addressed them. "We have a permit beginning at 8:00 this morning and until 8:00 tonight. We will leave this area as clean as we found it. You may come back tomorrow."

"You hear that boys?" he yelled to his comrades. "We're not invited to their picnic. Unfriendly, I'd call that."

Josef didn't take his eyes off the eyes of the leader, who looked away and saw Josephine.

"What's *she* all got up for, a carnival?" His buddies laughed.

Justin, standing next to Josef said in a clear voice for all the intruders to hear, "*She...*" and he counted to 10 slowly to himself, "...is my wife." He held his stick in a relaxed posture but even a casual look could see that it was ready for use. He kept his eyes on the leader's eyes, who quickly checked Josef and found his eyes equally fixed on his. He turned to his fellows and said with disgust, "This here's a simply boring, b-o-r-i-n-g party. I bet we can find more excitement anywhere but here". With that he got on his ATV and started the engine. The others did the same, and all made a show of wheelies and a lot of noise and dust as they left.

All remained still until they were out of sight and hearing, and then the tension broke into comments and conversations.

Joan turned to Sam. "I've told you about my study of courage and how I plan to fit that into my future. My father and yours have just given me a foundation beyond any theory."

Chapter Six – Wonderful to Behold

"Josephine, I can't thank you enough. It's amazing. The way you're dressed, speaking his language, showing him the dance from your homeland, getting him to join you with arm movements... but the grand touch was when you helped him stand up and shuffle in time to the music. He smiled, Josephine, a big, bright, happy smile. You did it. Josephine, it's a miracle for my first appointment of the day. I've never seen anything like it!" Linda sat back in a comfortable chair in a corner of the guest lounge where they had some privacy. "Now what do I do to follow up? If he can do all that in one session, after he's done absolutely nothing for weeks, think what he could accomplish with regular movement!"

"Linda, Benjamin speaks English very well, as you know, but let me teach you a few simple expressions in Swahili and let's start with one short and easy dance. I can teach it to you right now and you can record the music on your phone to practice later. I'll join you for the beginning of your next session, then explain that I have to leave but that he's in good hands with you. This way I'll transfer to you authority and endorsement. I'll teach you a greeting from me that you can give each time, and let me know how he's doing and tell him that you're letting me know. Most of all, just be yourself. You know what you're doing and what you want for his benefit, so have confidence; you have my confidence in you and soon you'll have his, too. Now, let's move a couple of chairs and dance." Linda caught on very quickly, and Josephine taught her a Swahili expression for encouragement and approval that she could use whenever he did well. Linda practiced that, too, while they danced. After just a little while Linda was having fun. Dancing was easy for her. Breaking through personal barriers was a challenge, but soon she absorbed Josephine's confidence.

After they finished their session, as they were getting ready to leave, Linda asked, "Josephine, Mom told me that you were named after Saint Josephine Bakhita. You have a wonderful namesake and I think you honor her in your life."

"Thank you, Linda. That means a lot to me because she is a very important person in my life. Very few in this country have heard of her. As you probably know, because I imagine you read about her life, she was enslaved as a young child in Africa and treated very, very cruelly for many years. Yet, she came through all that with strength, courage, and great kindness. I stay in touch with my family in Uganda, but I also stay in touch with her memory and spirit. She is my guide, especially when problems seem overwhelming and I am discouraged.

Here is a website with some more important expressions in Benjamin's language. Kwa heri, Linda."

"Kwa heri, Josephine."

With a light heart filled with hope, more than you might think a simple dance for improved therapy could give, Linda hurried to her next two appointments. Her next session with Benjamin was what was most on her mind, however.

Josef had no classes that morning, and he Miriam were having a cup of tea at the small table by their bay window in the kitchen, he in his running clothes, she in her 'comfortables'. They watched the two doves on a branch in the ash tree in their front yard.

"I wonder why they don't come down to eat. I filled the feeder and water dish," Josef idly noted, but Miriam heard the very slight edge to his voice.

"They have their reasons. Maybe they're not hungry. Maybe they're waiting for more warmth so they can move more easily. Maybe they've seen a predator we haven't noticed... Josef, what's on your mind?"

"You can always tell, can't you?" There was a long pause, but Josef relaxed because he was going to talk about it.

"I've been leading students in class for as long as I can remember, but leading a family is different. I don't know exactly how or why or what adjustments I should make. It's not the same as when the children were young. We used to say, 'Come on kids, get your jackets; we're going to the zoo,' and that was that. When they became teenagers, it became more challenging because I didn't always know how to talk to them. Personal relationships with my family are so different than professional relationships with students, and I know I haven't always made the switch easily. Now as adults, they really don't need or want my help very much. Oh, I know they love me and they know I love them, but sometimes I feel more distant than I want. How do I make sense out of all this? Miriam, what do you think I should do?"

Miriam waited a moment, sipped her tea, doodled a bit on a sheet of notepaper always handy wherever they were.

"Joseph, you're asking a very important set of questions. I sometimes struggle with being a mother at a new stage of their growth, and this is true even in their 20s. We want to be relaxed and casual and open yet keep proper boundaries. We want to honor their independence, yet we really want to be needed as we were when they were younger. We want to allow them the freedom they deserve yet guide them away from choices that might be mistakes, no matter how old they get. I know all parents have to work with these issues, but when it comes down to individual personalities there's no rulebook for parents for every situation, every mood, every hidden sensibility or sensitivity.

There is an important option that I figured out."

Josef realized that his wife understood him. He was listening. He kept quiet and waited.

"And you just did it. Keep silent. If we're too quick to rush in, too quick to believe we understand something that may only be the tip of something with long roots, too quick to add words to feelings already complicated, we may inadvertently be clumsy and trounce the seedlings reaching for the weeds. And you know that seedlings can be mixed in with mature growth and not easily seen and need a careful step aside while a large weed may need a two-handed pull. Silent waiting can sometimes, maybe even often, allow to be revealed to us the nature of what's before us.

Josef took a long pull at his tea, put the cup down without a sound, took a deep breath, let out a sigh, and said, "That's wonderful imagery, Miriam. That perspective, those insights, come from you so easily. You're a natural. I'm thinking I am more clumsy than you are. I thought I was practicing allowing more 'wait time' before moving forward. For quite a while I've felt something missing, but I don't know what it is."

Miriam leaned forward. "Josef, dear, you are very knowledgeable and very good with words. Maybe too good. Are you preparing what you're going to say while you're waiting?"

Josef leaned back, rubbed the top of his head, then his face with both hands.

"You know, I really am. You, and others, have told me that I'm too much the teacher all the time, that I lecture too readily. I seem to believe that my job is to bring 'light into darkness' for everyone about everything…"

"No, don't start getting down on yourself. You have a rich storehouse of knowledge, of wisdom, and are a generous soul who loves to share that wisdom. You clearly care about other people and want them to do well. No getting down on yourself allowed. It distracts from insights to be gained." Miriam said this with a smile and a gentle hand on his arm.

"There is something I'd like you to think about, Josef. I know it would a risk, a challenge rather, but suppose during a moment of silence you did not prepare anything to say. Suppose you simply observed. Maybe you take your own thoughts too seriously and overlook what's going on with others in that exact moment. The situation may have changed since the conversation began. We've talked about the progression of a deepening conversation, how trust is built one moment, one subtle signal, at a time. Those simple doves on that branch are changing one moment at a time. Maybe they do something we consider unexpected, but to them it's quite sensible. So much more, people. Let's both do this. Let's explore, let's allow insight to develop in that silence before we respond, no matter how excited or how irritated we are. Remember, consciously or not, the other person is observing us and sees in us the mood change, the feeling shift, and is adjusting quickly, often without even being conscious of it."

"Whew! Miriam, I married a genius. I think you're right on all counts. Would it be alright with you if I went for a quick run? I need to get all this integrated all the way down to my toes." And Josef laughed, a short but rich and happy laugh. He was on his way, out the door and into the sky.

Miriam laughed, too. She knew what a 'short run' could mean when he was like this. Josef's run turned out to be quite a long one. Conviction and resolution had increased with his steps. He ran down to the woodlands along the river. The path through sandy soil was packed after the recent rain. There were still some lingering storm clouds, but they brought only beauty with no threat of high winds and rain. He found a large, welcoming tree and rested. He was tired, a very good tired.

Pure rest never lasted long with Josef. Feelings and words began to appear. He took the hint and started to work out a song on note cards he always carried, 'just like Sam' he thought affectionately. After some revisions he decided to record it later so he could listen to it and remember this occasion, these learnings, this growth, these changes he wanted to make in himself, for himself, for others, too.

<u>Respite on the Trail</u>
I was helped; my heart rejoices. Psalm 28
How do I change and still be me,
honor and accept signals I see,
not fall back endlessly stuck
in those inclinations that rule so much,
holding fast, yet letting go,
relating in ways beyond those I know.
More and more we can become so close.
Yet any gain will surely be slow,
trying and relying on a breath of trust
for guiding and finding what might be for us,

> *grateful for those opportunities*
> *of not-alone receptivity.*
> *Respite in the woods brings home again*
> *living outward is who I am.*
> *The river full, the season's change,*
> *the trail hard-packed after rain,*
> *sky over all and towering clouds*
> *finding faith and blessings of God.*
> *Keepsakes and change found in the woods;*
> *answers abound from the reach of God.*
> *Clouds within sky bringing rain,*
> *the solid earth is wet but the same,*
> *the river sparkles and flows massively,*
> *I will change, yet still be me.*

Josef was now ready to go home. He wanted to sing his song for Miriam.

Farther downstream, in a small, secluded opening by that river sat Sam and Joan, the third time in as many days they came to "their place".

They couldn't always hold hands around other people but here they could, and more. They lay side-by-side, Sam's arm around her, Joan's head on his chest.

The two always-busy highly talkative young adults had talked themselves dizzy ever since the picnic. Now they simply breathed and watched the same clouds that Josef saw, clouds of darkness and of light, clouds that moved quickly and close and those much higher that held still. Those that changed shape, some disappearing.

"Clouds like feelings and moods come quickly and go

while our heartbeats together move surely and slow
when they rest in the love that we finally know."

"Mmm, mmm," Joan affirmed with a peaceful smile.

Neither spoke. A breeze ruffled Joan's hair. Sam gently duplicated the breeze and almost whispered, "My parents are happy for us. They say I'm pre-occupied with a person instead of ideas and thoughts and projects, that I'm too filled with the present to be so intent on developing the future."

"Mmm, mmm. Sam, my parents say pretty much the same thing about me, but a little differently. They saying I'm *being* more than *thinking* and it is indeed wonderful to behold. That's my mom's expression, but Dad nods and says, 'Yes, indeed. Yes, indeed.' Sam, I know that sometime we have to get on with our lives, school and all that. But let's not be in a hurry."

""Mmm, mmm," was all he could manage to say.

Chapter Seven – From a Full Heart

Joan knew they were well past mile five. She was much faster than her mother, but Josephine could run all day it seemed.

"Mom, how about a rest?"

They walked a bit, then eased into some shade with a good bed of pine needles. Both were quiet, except for pounding hearts, some deep breaths, and the sound of water with electrolytes going down in short intervals.

"Mom, can we talk about sex?"

"Sure."

"As you know, Sam will be graduating next month and is still deciding between two job offers. I'll be going right into a master's program with my three-year bachelor's degree that you and Dad encouraged. As soon as Sam decides, we'll announce our engagement. When he's settled into a job with a promising future, we plan to be married."

"Yes, Dear…"

"Well, I'm working up to it. It's a bit sensitive…" Joan took a deep breath.

"Sam and I have pledged to wait until marriage for our sexual relations, but… it is sooo difficult sometimes. I need some words of wisdom and encouragement…"

Josephine took a swallow from her second water bottle.

"I know, Joan. Your father and I were young, too. We waited, and it was difficult, and our courtship wasn't as long as yours. You and Sam are doing the right thing. You will recognize that even more as time goes on. Trust God, the purity of your love and your pledge, and each other. Run a lot."

Joan laughed. She laughed until she cried.

"Good advice, Mother, dear. But not easy. Sam is holding up well, pretty much. He doesn't put any pressure on me at all. I can tell it's difficult for him, too."

They were both quiet for a few minutes, then her mother said, "I hope Sam is talking with his father about this. There are some differences between a man and woman in this matter, with some responsibilities identical and some different for each.

There is something that you can do that Sam can't, based on your nature as a female. There's about a week each month when your sex drive will be stronger, due to ovulation. There are methods within natural family planning that can guide you to determine that. With that knowledge you and Sam can have a plan for that time."

That made perfect sense to Joan. She had not thought of that. She gave her mother a big hug. "Thanks, Mom. Hope increases with a good plan, I always say!"

Josephine jumped up and yelled, "Bet you can't catch me," knowing full well that she could.

Just about the time that Joan got to her feet and ran off in pursuit, Sam and his dad had pulled into some shade on the lake and were idling their kayaks. They had been in the water ever since breakfast and were tired and hungry and having a snack at the turn-around point.

"Dad, I'm running into some rough water I'd like to talk about." His Dad had a mouthful of food, but Sam could see his openness and started right in. "As you know, Joan and I are completely committed to each other, and that includes waiting until we're married before sex." He watched Dad for any sign of uneasiness. Seeing none, he continued, "Like most things, that's a lot easier said than done. I'm keeping pretty steady on course, but sometimes the rough water seems about to capsize me. I get a grip on the water flowing over me and turn just in time to avoid big trouble, but sometimes I'm afraid I might not make it through the next wave. Any thoughts?"

"Son, I really like your imagery. It fits the situation very well. I do have a few thoughts for you to consider.

First, and this sounds so simple, but it might help, why don't each of you write your pledge to each other briefly, then read it to each other when you're alone." He gave Sam a minute to reflect on that, and before he went on he was mindful of

Miriam's suggestions and watched Sam's face carefully and waited.

"I like that idea. I'll suggest it to Joan." When he nodded, Josef knew it was OK to continue.

Second, it can help to remember that as the man, you have unique responsibilities in a relationship. (Let's talk about the unique opportunities another time.) Joan is counting on your strength and resoluteness for the type of leadership that falls to you. Do you know what I mean?"

Sam looked a bit unsure. "No. I feel caught without a paddle." Sam always did like analogies, metaphors, all figures of speech.

Hesitatingly he said, "I think you may mean that I've got to be the anchor, that Joan is counting on me to be sure and true to our commitment, no matter how the winds blow and the waves surge. That she can relax and trust me. And believe me, she's doing her part. She's a woman of strong morals and character and she keeps her word. But I can see that sometimes she gets fluttery, like a kayak that's bouncing too much and having a hard time keeping to course."

"Sam, I want to leave the imagery for a while and say that sometimes you just have to reassure Joan that you love her and trust her and that you two can get through anything together.

I'm going to tell you something very personal. Your mom and I remember, and will always remember, our honeymoon. It was one of the most significant times of our lives, because we waited. The wait was a challenge, a purification, a trial, but it lapsed into faint memory compared to the honeymoon. You're welcome to share that story with Joan if you think it will help. You can even talk to your mother about all this. Believe me, she understands.

And finally, but of great importance, you will say 'In the name of God, I, Sam, take you, Joan, to be my wife, to have and to hold from this day forward, for better, for worse, for richer, for poorer, in sickness and in health, to love and to cherish, until we are parted by death. This is my solemn vow.' Sam, saving yourselves for each other in marriage will contribute greatly to the strength of the commitment to honor and keep that lifelong solemn vow."

Unknown to Sam and Joan, and none of their business, John and his father and Sue and her mother had very similar conversations just the previous week. They went like this.

John: "Dad, Sue and I are thrilled to be engaged. There's a glow within and around us. We've promised ourselves to each other for marriage, and that includes sexual restraint until then. Like most young people our age, I expect, we struggle with that sometimes. We talk about it, but seem to have run out of what more we can say. Sue's going to talk to her mother like I'm talking to you in hopes of some guidance."

Justin: "Thank you, John, for trusting me enough to discuss this. Our engagement was about as long as yours, so I can relate to your feelings and struggles. Hopefully I can help you know that you're not alone in this. Trust that this will make you stronger and strengthen your commitment to marriage and build your confidence as you and Sue go through your first great personal challenge as a couple.

I have two suggestions. First, pray by yourself before every time you will be with Sue, then together as you start any time alone pray and renew your full commitment to each other.

Second, your mom and I will make our cabin available to you, Sam, and Donald in any weekend of your choosing, but I would set a time when conversations with their fathers are still fresh. Those are two young men, I believe, who will understand your situation very well, and it wouldn't surprise me if you each could contribute ideas, insights, and strength to each other."

John: "Dad, I feel your encouragement and will remember it. Those are suggestions that can make a difference for me, and I will follow up on them."

True to his word, John took his father's suggestions to heart. He and Sue became more prayerful and it showed in their maturity and strengthened resolve. Within a week he talked to Donald who got out his calendar on the spot and told John he would clear either of the next two weekends, or any time that would work for him and Sam. Donald suggested that John be the one to talk to Sam, telling him that his brother was on board. He thought that would build their relationship.

Only a few days after Sam's conversation with his dad, John invited Sam on a short but steep hike, and at an overlook mentioned his dad's idea. Sam responded, "John, I think it's a good idea, but I've never done anything like this. Besides my family and Joan, I've never been close to anyone."

John felt kindly to Sam's straightforward and innocent manner and said, "Sam, have you stopped to think that you will be my brother-in-law? Isn't that family?"

Sam laughed. "Ah, yes! Count me in." They shook on it.

The only open link in the family soon closed when Sue's mother said one day when they were baking several loaves of bread and no one else was at home, "Sue, you are a very confident and accomplished young lady, but I know there is one topic you are uneasy discussing."

At first Sue didn't know what her mother meant, and then she did. She became a bit flustered and started cleaning all the surfaces in the kitchen with her back to her mother.

"Sue, I'm not prying, but I think it's time we had a mother-daughter talk. Let's sit on the patio. I just made a fresh jar of iced spearmint-chamomile tea, your favorite."

With both reluctance and some eagerness, for Sue knew that this was necessary, she joined her mother in the warm sunshine.

"Do you remember when we first talked about sex?" Sue nodded. At the end of our talk you said, 'Mom, that's beautiful.'

You were so right. I gave you a big hug then, and here's a big hug now."

The embrace reminded Sue just how safe she felt in her mother's arms.

"You and John love each other and are true to each other in all ways, including waiting for marriage for the part of your relationship that belongs only to your marriage." Sue nodded. Miriam continued, moving slowly and with sensitivity for Sue's uneasiness, which was fading, she noticed.

I wanted to talk about this because your father and I were young and in love and engaged, too. I had never been engaged or married or with a man in any way except a handshake. I was eager, willing, naïve. The engagement was a signal to me that marriage was coming, something I wasn't sure would ever happen for me. I was so much hidden away into books and studies and writing and religion that I thought I was destined to be alone always. But God had another plan, for which I am eternally grateful. Your dad has been the gift of my life, which brought the gifts of you and your brothers. Sex was and is part of those gifts, Sue, and I can tell you that waiting during the engagement was as necessary as it was difficult. I was fully committed to keeping my virginity until we were married and then giving it to your father unreservedly in the fullness of my love, but it was difficult. We made it, Sue, and you and John can make it too. Rest assured, dear daughter, that we have been down that path before and though it isn't always smooth walking, the destination is most worth it. Your father and I still remember and refer to our honeymoon as a high point of our lives and of our marriage."

Sue hadn't said a word, but her eyes and ears and heart were open all the way. She got up and went to her mom. Their hug brought back all the hugs of her life, especially the one her mother had given her the first time they talked about sex.

Miriam knew the hug was from a full heart.

Chapter Eight – Tears and Laughter in God's Eye

Time can beat as slowly as a heart at peace or loneliness, or seem to rush like a river building speed downhill toward a waterfall. So much of time in both ways had gone by since the 'grand picnic'.

At the overlook that had been their resting place in previous years, Josef waited quietly. He knew his friend needed to talk. They hadn't spoken since greetings in the parking lot more than two hours ago.

"Josef, my brother, I'm glad we could meet here. We haven't hiked to this place together since well before Rivka died. I've been a recluse, I know, but I'm lost without her. She was my purpose for living. She did get to see little Mary Rebecca born to Max and Phoebe and that meant more to her than words can ever say. She held her, wondered and prayed over her, and cried because she could feel her time was short. It wasn't long afterwards that her decline steepened, as if she had waited for the baby and now it was alright to leave. In the end, she simply said my name over and over, sighed and went away.

Josef, I'm not a writer like you, like so many in your family. I want to read these two lines to you. It will help in my unburdening, perhaps.

When I was with Rivka at the end, I remembered and re-read the poem that Celia wrote through Rivka's eyes. I wanted Rivka to speak to me, but she could not. I wanted to hold her in my arms and tell her I loved her, but she was so frail and easily disturbed if moved. I held her and said over and over, 'Rivka, I love you'. There was only her breath slowly coming to an end. I didn't think she could hear me, but then she said, once: Isaac. That was all. That was her end. Josef, I cried non-stop until I couldn't cry or even breathe any more. Every time I could, I cried some more. Max and Phoebe and your family were tremendously helpful. I couldn't have lived otherwise. I couldn't eat. I didn't know what to do. I was lost, abandoned, alone.

One night, after I finally slept for several hours at a stretch, I awoke thinking of Rivka. A line came to me. I got up and wrote it, but didn't know what else to do. Then I thought of Rivka, she was so religious. She loved God. She trusted God. I wrote the second line, and that was all. I felt somehow reassured, somehow it felt like I had Rivka again, that I could share her memory with God. Here are the two lines."

Isaac took a small, stained and wrinkled paper out of his shirt pocket. With a shaking hand and voice, and a long pause after the first line, he read:

*When you are no longer with me, and I am just a sigh
and then I lose my breath, I'll be a memory in God's eye.*

Isaac didn't cry. He looked at his friend and smiled and said, "Do you see, Josef? God and I have Rivka in our eyes, in our hearts, forever. I am not alone. God is with me, and he loves Rivka, too.

Then Isaac cried.

Josef put his hand on Isaac's shoulder, firmly. Isaac composed himself and said, "The last time we were here, my brother, I was so saddened with the descent of Rivka into her disease and I asked you for a favor. I ask you again. Would you please catch me up with every member of the family? I have lost touch with everyone except Max and Phoebe and Mary Rebecca. I have been empty for too long. I need to know about those I love, please.

Josef knew he had time. The weather was fair and unlike so many of his days, he had nothing for which to hurry. So he began: "Isaac, the last two recollections by the family are of you and Rivka at the picnic at the lake and at Mary Rebecca's Christening. Those were a couple of years ago, and I'll begin there.

Donald and Celia gave birth to Joseph Donald, a nine-pound wrestler. It was about the time Phoebe gave birth." Isaac gave a rare smile to this image of a new-born wrestler.

"Everyone enjoys talking about the grand friendship Joseph and Mary will have as they grow up together." Another smile from Isaac. Josef relaxed and became lighter.

Celia is in the early stages of another pregnancy, and so far the baby is growing well and Celia is as happy as she could be. Donald is wearing fatherhood proudly. He has had another significant promotion. Like Max, he takes his duties very seriously. Celia is always telling him to relax, enjoy, laugh. He worries too much, that son of mine.

John and Sue are very happily married now. They, too, love each other dearly. John completed a very concentrated course of studies for certification and is now teaching fifth grade. He loves it. His father, Justin, sees it and is so glad that he gave his son the go-ahead for his dream.

Sam and Joan are such a delight. I've always said each one is 'strikingly unique', and that is as true in marriage as it was in their single state.

Sam has a very good job with a hospital system using his interests and degree in industrial-organizational psychology. He loves working with the principles and research methods he intuitively grasps and has learned to improve work environments including job performance, communication, and safety. He still visits Max's business and the two of them very much enjoy figuring ways for continuous improvement. He's able to support Joan in her advanced studies in sociology and they're hoping to work together someday. They're not able to start a family yet, so natural family planning is an important part of their lives.

For the men, Max, Sam, Donald, John, there's developed a wonderful camaraderie. They get together regularly. It strengthens them as men, as husbands, as fathers, a great blessing. Justin and I are invited to join them often. They seem to value our age and wisdom!

For the women, a similar relationship developed beginning in this way. John's mother, Josephine, worked with Linda in her dance/movement therapy to help Benjamin, a marathoner from Africa in the U.S. as a graduate student. He was badly injured in a fall and demoralized. With their help he recovered his strength, most of his fitness, and his confidence to start running competitively again as a result of their combined efforts. He doesn't care if he's ever as fast as he once was because he's so happy to be running again. Linda runs with him, side by side. They are growing closer day by day. Josephine and Linda informally started meeting with Miriam to discuss women's issues because they respect her so much, and gradually Celia, Sue, and Phoebe joined them. This has been as much of a blessing to the women as the men's group is to the men."

This was a lot for Isaac to think about, so Josef took a break to stretch. Isaac needed that, too, and when he bowed with a hand-wave aimed up the trail, without a word the two old-timers headed toward the peak where they knew they could continue the conversation while looking out over the world.

As the men climbed steadily, the woman's group was close to ending its monthly morning meeting. Miriam spoke up.

"I know how much we all enjoy and benefit from getting together, and Josef tells me the men feel the same way about their group. How about joining forces for a day in the mountains with the children? Josef and I could list all the topics each group has discussed, and which ones have been most important. We could draft a combined list that we all might like to talk about, then bring that list back to each group for final thoughts before we decide the topics for the day. What do you think?"

Phoebe was the first to respond. "I think it's a great idea. I wonder if it might help for there to be a brief women's session and men's session before the end of the day for each group to summarize their thoughts, in particular for the men to list what was most helpful to have heard from the women and vice versa."

The women liked everything they were hearing.

With shyness, Linda quietly added, "How would you feel if I asked Dad to ask the men if it'd be alright to include Benjamin?"

The women smiled at this request and said, "Absolutely a good idea!" Linda felt a rush of gladness for these women in her life.

Celia offered to watch the young ones. "I can imagine that Donald will write a summary, or report, or article about our conference so I'll know all about everything I miss."

Generosity is always inspirational. Phoebe said, "I'll take turns with Celia, and I think we should give the men an opportunity to volunteer for childcare, too, at the first annual Living Well Conference. I'm sure Max would be glad to."

With general laughter, everyone approved the name and the ideas.

That evening after dinner Linda brought up something very important to her. "Dad, before you talk to the men about the LivingWell Conference, (Josef couldn't help but smile at the name, with no small amount of good pride), I wanted to ask you if you'd ask them if it'd be alright to invite Benjamin."

She was expecting one of his long pauses, but right away he said, "Sure. I think it's a good idea." Then came a pause as he looked at Linda for a moment. "You're rather fond of that young man, aren't you?"

Now it was Linda's turn to take a moment before she answered. The answer was a well-known 'yes', but this might be the time to say more. "Yes, very much. Dad, I've never been in a deep and true love before, but this sure seems like it's going in that direction. You know I'm kind of a shy and reticent person (Joseph showed a faint smile and nodded gently, for this, too, was very well known), but I find that I can talk more openly with Benjamin than anyone. He's an amazing listener. I can talk long and he listens long with not the slightest interruption, thinks about what I've said, and then like shooting an arrow straight at a bull-eye (Linda loved long-bow archery), he gives me an answer or makes a comment so pithy that I can think about it for a long while. Dad, we read Scripture together and discuss it, pray together, and of course run together. Where else in this world could I find someone like Benjamin. His feelings about marriage are of its sacredness and permanence, like mine.

Our only difference is that he wants a really big family. I asked him, 'How big'. He smiled and said, 'a dozen children'. Not eight, or nine, ten or eleven. A dozen! He's quite sure. Dad, I don't know if I can do that. I mean, how do I even think about having that many children? I mentioned to him my misgivings and he said, 'Linda, there are many orphans in my country and many children, even in my village, who don't have enough to eat, who are being raised by relatives rather than by parents. We could have as many children as you can and adopt the rest'. He said it so matter-of-factly. He's so simple-minded for such a brilliant man. Maybe it's better to say his mind makes complex matters simple!

He's wants to be a civil engineer to design the roads and bridges that his part of his country needs. He wants me to live there with him and a growing family until he gets bridges and roads in place, then he says we can bring the children here for an education and he'll establish his career in the U.S. Dad, how do I think about all this?"

Now Josef did pause, got another cup of coffee, and stood at the large window overlooking the garden and fruit trees while he settled his thoughts.

When he returned to the table, he called for Miriam to join them and briefly filled her in on Linda's dilemma. Linda waited with shallow, rapid breathing and no small amount of apprehension, for she had no idea what her parents would say.

Finally, her mother looked at her father, who smiled and nodded in his characteristic way, then she said with his apparent agreement, "Linda, we will certainly miss you and you know, we've never been to Africa. I've always wanted to see elephants in their natural habitat. (Linda had always wondered about the large carving of a family of elephants hanging in her parents' bedroom. It came to mind now.)

Linda didn't know whether to laugh, or cry, to withdraw into silence and leave the room or jump up and dance on the table, so she just sat, stunned. At last, she walked slowly to her mother, put her arms around her, her head on her mother's shoulder, and whispered, "I love you, Mom. I realize now my decision was in front of me all the time, in Benjamin. I lacked the courage to accept what I knew was right, what was for me and my heart.

He gives me a full heart, Mom. I will follow him wherever he goes." She went to her father. "Dad, I miss you already, just thinking about this, miss you terribly, and it makes me afraid. Benjamin is a good man, Dad, a strong and faithful man. He will take good care of me, I know. I will be safe and happy with him… and with our 12 children." Linda laughed. Her mother and father laughed. For just a second, Linda saw in her mind the elephants in the carving laughing, too. That reminded her of something she had written in response to this overwhelming situation she was in, modeled on what Isaac had written when he was overwhelmed at Rivka's death. Phoebe had shared it with her with Isaac's blessing. Linda put her lines to a short melody and now sang it for her parents.

In all that now shall come to me, I will both laugh and cry
and keep all my deep feelings, living always in God's eye.

Josef touched Miriam's hand. They interlaced their fingers in a gratitude that had no words.

Chapter Nine – The Living Well Conference

Josef did even better than Linda asked. He asked the men if Benjamin could join them for their regular get-togethers. Without hesitation they unanimously assented. Benjamin proved to be a quiet but significant addition to their union. When they discussed the conference scheduled for next Spring at John's parents' cabin in the mountains, it was simply assumed that Benjamin would be there. He fit in to the men's regular activities as smoothly as the second mile in a long race, and it was evident to everyone that he and Linda were slowly but surely headed toward engagement and marriage.

The weekend for the conference, an upgrade in scope from the wonderful family get-togethers they'd enjoyed over the years, was set for Josef's 60th birthday. He felt honored. Everyone made plans to be there; they made such a point of giving a special invitation to Isaac that he accepted with humility and elation.

Weather at the mountain cabin in the Spring could be something to contend with, so they all planned for wet or dry, warm and humid or cold and windy. Because the dirt road would get slippery after heavy rain, those without four-wheel drive trucks planned to ride with those who had them. Donald took his job as "emergency preparedness coordinator" very seriously because the stream that flowed near the house had overflowed in the past, and once the log-and-plank bridge from the cabin to the road became impassable. He made plans to bring in more than enough foodstuffs beforehand in the unlikely possibility of being stranded for a time, and the shed was filled with firewood. The well was cleaned, the electric pump checked with the freshwater storage tank and spare tank to be filled after the last frost. Extra tools would supplement those kept at the cabin in case they needed to repair the bridge or the road. Donald knew that in all likelihood everything would be just fine, but he was never one to rule out the unexpected.

Personal lives, of course, had to go on with their rich complexity, their eventful and uneventful days and weeks and months.

Isaac was a most welcome addition to the men's group. At first he was reluctant, feeling much the outsider, but the men were persistent. They prevailed upon him to host a meeting, believing he'd be more comfortable in his own house, and indeed he was. The abundant photographs of Rivka, Isaac, and baby Phoebe, as well as Rivka's favorite paintings and wall-mounted artifacts made by her mother, gave plenty of rich substance to the memories he shared. Afterwards, Josef said to the men at a brief tailgate meeting, "I'm glad you all were there to hear Isaac's stories. Although it was difficult for him in the beginning, I think it gave him a lot of healing. Did you notice how relaxed and outgoing he was before we left?" Yes, indeed they certainly did, and it opened the coming weeks for Isaac to comfortably and regularly join them.

Celia went overtime to give birth, to another boy, a robust 10-pounder they named Nicholas Maximus. Everyone said he was almost ready for field, court, or bike ride. Unfortunately, her milk wasn't enough, so it had to be supplemented daily with formula. Not too long before, Phoebe brought another little healthy girl into the world, named Clare Reva, the middle name being a diminutive for Rivka. Although so much of their marriage included Phoebe's family, Max was generous and supportive in every way. "Maximus," she said one day, "you are, indeed, the maximum of every quality I could ever hope for in a husband, a father for our daughters, a son-in-law for my father. I probably don't say that enough." This was an especially generous gesture, as her old depression had returned since the birth. She had a difficult pregnancy and was confined to bed for the last month, and Clare Reva was a month early besides. Her doctor had said, in a straightforward but kind way, "Phoebe, the risk for you to have another child is considerable. Please avoid pregnancy." It was hard on them both. Max was hoping for a boy sometime, but stays as lighthearted as he can to try to lift

Phoebe's sadness. He often says to her with such a smile that it always brings a grin to her face, "I'll get good at understanding girls, for sure!"

Sue and John are deliriously happy and blend their unique personalities well as any successfully married couple must. Sue gave up her childhood dream of serving aboard the USNS Mercy, realizing that it would be much more practical for her to be a nurse near home. With her love for children utmost in her mind, she decided to become a school nurse. She shares a full-time position at two schools, in one of which John teaches. The harmony which they both value and for which they actively strive now has a professional as well as personal dimension. Sue is in the early stages of her first pregnancy, but it's too early to know if she's carrying twins. All, especially Grandma Miriam, are certainly hopeful, though of course say nothing about it to Sue and John.

Linda and Benjamin had announced their engagement to toasts and "hurrahs". Benjamin's extraordinary powers of listening were quite apparent in the men's group as they all shared with him the joys and challenges of engagement. In the women's group, it was much the same with Linda, with none of the kidding and good-natured bantering of the men due to Linda's serious and private nature. In deference to her daughter's great modesty, Miriam had talked with her privately days before, providing the necessary outline and details on managing the closeness of engagement without the prerogatives of marriage. She made it comfortable, thorough, and as brief as such an important topic could be.

Joan had made it through her master's and doctoral studies in record time. She was working night and day, with great joy, on her dissertation: "Courage as Necessary Impetus for Conflict Resolution: Case Studies Across Continents". She was writing about families she knew, with permission and name changes of course. A trip to Uganda with Josephine had given her abundant comparison, contrast and surprising common ground across cultures. Although an extraordinary occurrence, Linda and

Benjamin had welcomed her into their plans for their honeymoon to his home country. Sam, who thought the term *Curiosity* should somehow be included in the dissertation's title, was going along as co-investigator. His employer gladly granted permission for an extended leave, and out of gratitude he had arranged to visit with hospital administrators in Nairobi, whom he hoped would welcome a "sister-city" relationship. He and his mother shared a love of elephants, and he would welcome a paid business trip anytime.

Expectations and excitement, planning and preparing for the Grand Weekend, as it was also called, grew in intensity and urgency as the time approached. All watched the weather reports. The 7-day forecast, usually quite accurate, showed a sizable storm entering the region. Unperturbed, Donald was a model of calmness and focus on preparedness. Everyone borrowed his confidence, secretly wishing for a "plan B" that wouldn't be as deflating as "postponement". Donald had none to offer, other than to celebrate at their large house which, with everyone's due respect, "just wouldn't be the same". Adventurers all, they checked their raingear, packed extra clothes, food and personal supplies, and hoped for the best.

With just a few days to go, the greatest threat of the storm veered to the east, so with a sigh of relief, emergency preparations still in force, everyone felt that everything was ready for a memorable weekend.

Because Josef's birthday coincided with a three-day weekend, Friday morning found trucks loaded, adults down to babies ready to go.

The distance to Justin and Josephine's family cabin was less than three hours usually, with the last stretch on the narrow dirt road the slowest by far. With new ruts and rocks and babies on board it took even longer this time, but all arrived in good form. They were glad that the "partly sunny" forecast was holding true, but that also meant partly cloudy and some of those were certainly storm clouds. They knew they were in for some rain, "but that won't dampen our spirits", punned Sam. There were smiles, but everyone glanced at the sky for the umpteenth time as they brought the supplies into the cabin.

A fine meal was grilled for them all, with Sam and Sue, John and Joan leading the cooking duties. Because of the breeze and clouds it was quite cool, so a fire was in order. With roasted marshmallows and endless stories, there was happiness and contentment and the afternoon slipped uneventfully into evening. With the temperature dropping, mothers and babies went inside first. Those kept outside with close-of-day chores were glad to find a fire in the fireplace and hot water in the kettles when they went inside. It was a time for the singing of favorites and simple guessing games to figure which one of the group was described in clever and often funny clues. It was a time of peace and gladness for love of family and friends. And then the winds came.

Justin, Isaac, and Donald, the men in team one, moved quietly around the cabin with reassuring nonchalance and remarks while they placed candles and lanterns in safe but easy reach of the adults, cleared space for firewood near the fireplace and woodburning stoves, retrieved extra blankets, and spent time with the young mothers and babies.

Josef, Sam, Max, John and Benjamin, team two, went outside in their rain jackets to shutter the house, fetch extra firewood, bring the trucks to high ground near the cabin and face them toward the road and bridge, and check surroundings for any gear left outside. John took the lead around his mountain home. Josef, Justin, and Benjamin stayed outside to study the sky and talk about the bridge.

The wind was strong enough to bend trees and its sounds in the forest and around the cabin could be heard inside.

In team three, Miriam and Josephine helped Celia and Phoebe with the little ones accompanied by soothing songs.

Team four, Linda, Sue, and Joan prepared the evening meal, planned in advance.

There was very little talking. Everyone was confident that they were well prepared and their trust in one another was complete. Justin and Josephine had built the cabin strong. They felt secure.

Low dark clouds scudded up the valley and higher up storm clouds churned their ice and water ominously. From his truck, Josef retrieved his battery powered computer and portable internet connection box and set them up on the tailgate.

"This weather site gives hourly updates of wind velocity and direction, air pressure, humidity and amount of expected precipitation, and size and location of a storm in radar imagery. We can track what's above us and around us. Since the last time I looked, the storm closest to us has moved to the northeast, though a good-sized part of it is with us right now."

Benjamin didn't know the area and asked, "So what's the likelihood of flooding where we are. I remember that you said the bridge to the road was flooded out once."

Justin answered, "Yes, that was a few years ago. The stream forks about 100 yards above us. The fork that goes west carries more water to a larger development downstream. At the fork there are large boulders. John and I made a rock sled and brought the ones you see shoring up the bank by the bridge. The logs supporting the planks held well, but some planks had to be replaced. We dredged the stream on the uphill side, but it's filled in again by now, I imagine.

But that was before the forest fire on two peaks a few miles upstream. The burn scars are extensive. We haven't had a real big storm since, but as you know those scars have no growth to retain rainwater and will shed it quickly downhill. I also watched the forecasts very closely for the past two weeks and agree with Josef that it seemed the storm would bypass us this weekend, or at worst skirt us to the east with only some normal Spring rain here. All that's changed very quickly. I think we're in for a good soaking."

Benjamin considered all this and said, "Donald's arranged enough provisions so we could hole up for a week. We might get sick of rice and beans, but I wouldn't worry."

Justin agreed. "As long as the bridge is here, we can get out quickly in an emergency and the road from here to Lakeview is passable, even in storms. West of us along the big fork usually gets the worst of it. But again, that's always been the case before the big fire."

Josef took the computer and internet box into their bedroom where he could watch the hourly updates, then rejoined the others.

Music and "merry camaraderie" as Sam called it, was the order of the day. It was long past bedtime for the children and young mothers who said a very tired, "Good night to all". Sam, John, Max and Benjamin sat up talking with the low firelight for company. Soon they, too, fell comfortably asleep in their sleeping bags.

During the night, Benjamin, who was alert in all but the deepest sleep, heard the continuous hard rain. Josef might not be worried, but he kept thinking of that bridge, their link with the outside world, and the babies. He heard the scurrying of mice, but paid no attention to that because Donald had insisted in hard, mouse-proof containers for all the food.

The morning dawned later in the mountains and hills around the cabin, but brought with it a thick green brightness from the sunshine and night's rain. Morning greetings and cheerfulness quickly shifted into concern when Celia noticed that the lid for the box with the baby formula hadn't been put on tight and mice had rummaged through all the packets and ruined them. Her first thought was the need for a trip to town, inconvenient but it would give her and Donald some time alone. Concern changed to alarm when Max came in with news that the bridge had been damaged.

Everyone was outside in minutes. "Oh, no! It can't be! What happened?!" Donald held Celia as Benjamin made an assessment.

"This boulder wasn't here last night. The swollen stream eroded the foundation for the uphill log and a crash from the boulder caused it to drop several inches. The bank is slippery and unstable, and with the planks tilted, we can't drive across the bridge until it's repaired. That will take more than a day or two. One good thing: it's on the roadside. We can sled rocks from where the stream forks."

Celia screamed, "My baby can't go two days without formula, and I don't have enough milk for him!"

The women rushed to her side. The men started planning, deciding which tools were needed, and who would do what.

Benjamin spoke. "I've got a block and tackle and plenty of strong rope in my truck. Max knows how to set it up. You'll need a strong tower for a hoist. You have a rock sled in the garage. While some of you are hauling big rocks, others can make ready the bank for reinforcement with the boulders. The block and tackle will lift the slumped log high enough to build a rock foundation under it. If we free the planks from that log, it will be easier. Those high-top fishing boots I saw in the shed will let you take turns in the stream prying out the spikes from the planks. It'll take a day or two or more for the stream to go down and slow down enough for you to do that. Meantime, build the hoist tower.

"A day or two!", Celia cried.

Benjamin was lacing up his running shoes and reaching for his backpack. "Celia, I can be back from Lakeview in a couple of hours, allowing for some mud. It's going to be OK."

A couple of voices said, "That's a long way, Benjamin!" "It's at least six miles each way!"

"Almost a half-marathon round trip. If the road isn't too muddy, I'll be back by lunchtime."

Celia and everyone watched with relief and gratitude as he walked over the one good log with heavy rushing water just inches below. He was surefooted but used his walking stick for balance because the broken bridge was shaking in the high, pulsing stream. From the other side he gave a smile, a wave, and he was gone.

"Celia, you can trust Benjamin. He's fast. And look what we found." Linda held up the one bag of baby formula that had not been chewed by the mice. Nicholas Maximus is OK until Benjamin gets back."

Celia hugged Linda for a long time. She was shaking more than the bridge.

The work began in earnest and continued non-stop all morning. The only conversation was related to tasks at hand. Lunch was the only break. Everyone noticed, but no one commented, that Benjamin was not back by lunch, nor even in the afternoon. Although nervous, Celia had enough for the baby for the day. Surely Benjamin would come before dark.

But the shadows were lengthening in the late afternoon and he was not back. Celia sat with Miriam and Phoebe in a back room. She felt very alone.

"I hear the pleasant conversations in the big room, the laughter, the singing. My baby may get very sick or die. No one understands. No one." Celia hid her face in her hands and sobbed.

"It's going to be alright, Celia," Phoebe reassured her. Benjamin will be back soon. We do understand."

"You don't understand!" Celia screamed, tears running down her face. Phoebe, you have just enough milk for Clare, so you can't help me. She's going to be OK. Nicholas is not going to be OK. Don't tell me you understand." Celia had never yelled at anyone. She had never lost her temper. She was known for her calmness, her self-assurance.

Miriam motioned for Phoebe to leave quietly. She sat still until Celia calmed down. "No one outside our immediate family knows, but I lost my brother when he was a little boy."

Celia jerked her head up, eyes wide open, still breathing shallow and fast. "What?" she exclaimed, shocked past her anger and fear.

"He was much younger, my only sibling. Our parents were still alive then, but mother was very ill. I took care of him as if I were his mother. I raised him. I loved him deeply and he loved me. He depended on me, but I wasn't there for him when he needed me. I used to meet him on his walk home from school because he had to use a neighborhood crosswalk, just one crosswalk, and the street wasn't busy. One day I wasn't there. He was hit by a car and died instantly. My sadness and guilt were overwhelming. Not long after that my mother died. Two years later, my father.

Celia, despite the immense sorrow and endless loneliness and longing, I found out how strong I was. Women are strong. Men have their way to be strong, but women have a different way. We endure, and it is deep. You will get through this, and we will get through it with you. And Celia, your baby is very healthy and strong. He will be fine. Benjamin will arrive soon."

Celia went to Miriam and hugged her a very long time. Then she snapped straight up. "Phoebe. I've got to apologize to Phoebe! She's had her loss, her sorrows. God have mercy," she prayed.

It was twilight when Benjamin came limping up the road. He crossed the wobbly bridge very slowly and carefully, for his pack was full with many containers of powdered formula, enough to last two weeks. He was strong as well as fast.

Everyone ran to greet him. Donald took his pack. Josephine handed him a sandwich and bottle of water. He sat on a bench and explained while he ate. "The stores in Lakeview were out of formula. I had to go to Crestview, but found what we need."

Celia covered his shoulders with a blanket, took his hands in hers and spoke to him quietly, "Benjamin, you saved my baby's life. We're stuck here longer than the one good bag of formula could last. Thank you. Thank you." She kissed him on the cheek. Donald helped him into the cabin.

Later, when he and Linda were alone on the porch, Benjamin said, "I ran the whole way, as fast as I could. Some parts of the road were not too bad. I was careful not to fall, but I haven't run that distance that fast since before my injury. My hip hurts." Without words, Linda helped him up and inside. He cleaned off the mud, ate and drank again, and didn't stir from a deep sleep until late the next morning, a morning of sunshine and clear skies.

After a breakfast of thanksgiving and celebration, friends and family gathered outside in a circle. It was Josef's birthday. Late to join came Celia and Phoebe, walking down out of the woods arm in arm. No one said a word as they took their babies from Miriam and Linda and sat side by side.

Donald stood in the center as master of ceremonies. At a signal, with smiling faces and laughing eyes everyone sang the birthday song with the final verse based on the one sung when Sam and Sue were born and which was sung also for Miriam's 50th birthday years ago.

Welcome birth-day to you,
Welcome birth-day to you,
Welcome birth-day dear father and grandfather Josef,
You've helped all our dreams come true!

Josef and Miriam kissed as everyone cheered. Donald handed his father his guitar, and in a strong, clear voice Josef sang to Miriam one of the many songs he had composed for her over the years. This was the first time anyone else had heard it. The only other sounds in the forest were the birds. Then he put down his guitar and stood up.

"Thank you for being here, for joining us, for being our family, all of you." Max and Phoebe knew he meant it for them, knew it was true, but appreciated hearing it.

"From all of us, thank you Justin and Josephine for the use of your beautiful cabin."

Josef collected his thoughts. "I've given a lot of thought to the title for this get-together, this "LivingWell" conference. The Livengoods Living Well. Sounds like a book title. We are one family, so I ask all of us to share the honorary name *LivingWell Family* in spirit and belonging, keeping your family names of course and your individual personalities, and yet belonging in one family with us just as we might use the expression The American Family in which we are all members.

Living well has different meanings for different people. For me it means living with integrity, honesty, fidelity to your spouses and family, and to the solid and eternal values of faith, hope, and love. It means preserving trust in God, yourselves, and each other, working through problems and honoring relationships in the midst of tensions and difficulties.

This weekend has been an experience in all of these core principles of living well.

Living well does not mean living without sadness or anger, worry or fear, doubt or failure. These occur within everyone's life. Living well means living through and getting above the pressure and pain that these can cause, sometimes in a gut-gripping way. May these kinds of troubles always lead us to an increase in sensitivity, compassion, and gratitude for all our many blessings.

One of the songs I wrote for Miriam is called *In All That Comes to Us*. I'd like to close my remarks by singing the last two lines to all of you, to each of you, changed just a bit for this occasion. I especially want to include someone whose illness prevents her from being with us, someone who has been such an important part of our family, whose faithfulness and courage have been an inspiration to me and to our children. We hope and pray that we will see her well and among us once again: our dear Aunt Tu.

In a voice quavering with emotion, Josef sang slowly and clearly:

*O LivingWell Family, our memories prove our love is true.
In all that comes to us, please know forever I love you!*

Unplanned, a receiving line formed for Josef. He spoke with each person, Miriam by his side.

Donald's planning and provisions served well the several days it took to rebuild the bridge, and on a day full of promise like the one that began their time together in the mountains, the full-to-overflowing entire LivingWell Family drove away with memories of love and strength and courage that would last a lifetime and be passed down for generations.

www.ingramcontent.com/pod-product-compliance
Lightning Source LLC
Chambersburg PA
CBHW041723070526
44585CB00006B/134